Building Slack Bots

Create powerful, useful, fast, and fun chat bots that make Slack better

Paul Asjes

PUBLISHING

BIRMINGHAM - MUMBAI

Building Slack Bots

First published: June 2016

Production reference: 1170616

Published by Packt Publishing Ltd.
Livery Place
35 Livery Street
Birmingham B3 2PB, UK.

ISBN 978-1-78646-080-6

www.packtpub.com

Credits

Author
Paul Asjes

Reviewer
Nicolas Grenié

Commissioning Editor
David Barnes

Acquisition Editor
Usha Iyer

Content Development Editor
Mehvash Fatima

Technical Editor
Siddhi Rane

Copy Editor
Roshni Banerjee

Project Coordinator
Kinjal Bari

Proofreader
Safis Editing

Indexer
Monica Ajmera Mehta

Graphics
Kirk D'Penha

Production Coordinator
Shantanu N. Zagade

Cover Work
Shantanu N. Zagade

About the Author

Paul Asjes started programming on his TI-83 calculator in high school and has been hooked ever since.

Specializing in JavaScript, he is always interested in staying up to date with the latest developments in the field. Currently, he is building universal full-stack apps with technologies such as React, Webpack, and Node when he's not spending far too much time on Slack.

Since his IRC days, he has been interested in chat bots and how they can be used. He has written several Slack bots to date, ranging from bots that facilitate playing games to bots that retrieve important business metrics.

I would like to thank my wife, Caitlin, for being my biggest fan, proofreader, and muse during the writing of this book.

About the Reviewer

Nicolas Grenié is a hacker-in-residence at 3scale, living between Barcelona and San Francisco.

Nicolas built his first website in 2000 using Microsoft Word and since then has not stopped learning about programming.

This API freak likes to try new languages and APIs all the time. He has built many integrations for Slack and Amazon Echo. He runs a good number of meetups in Barcelona about APIs, Meteor, and entrepreneurship.

When he isn't working, you have a good chance of finding him hacking side projects or enjoying a good craft beer. And, of course, as he is French, frogs and snails are part of his daily diet!

I want to thank Steven Willmott, the CEO of 3scale, and the entire 3scale team for giving me the inspiration and time to hack interesting projects and technology.

I also want to thank my parents and family for the positive learning environment they've built, letting me explore my passion and curiosity for technology.

www.PacktPub.com

eBooks, discount offers, and more

Did you know that Packt offers eBook versions of every book published, with PDF and ePub files available? You can upgrade to the eBook version at www.PacktPub.com and as a print book customer, you are entitled to a discount on the eBook copy. Get in touch with us at customercare@packtpub.com for more details.

At www.PacktPub.com, you can also read a collection of free technical articles, sign up for a range of free newsletters and receive exclusive discounts and offers on Packt books and eBooks.

https://www2.packtpub.com/books/subscription/packtlib

Do you need instant solutions to your IT questions? PacktLib is Packt's online digital book library. Here, you can search, access, and read Packt's entire library of books.

Why subscribe?

- Fully searchable across every book published by Packt
- Copy and paste, print, and bookmark content
- On demand and accessible via a web browser

Table of Contents

Preface   v

Chapter 1: Getting Started with Slack   1

    Introduction to Slack   1
    Slack as a platform   2
    The end goal   4
    Summary   4

Chapter 2: Your First Bot   5

    Preparing your environment   6
        Installing Node.js   6
        Installing the development tools using NPM   7
        Creating a new project   8
        Creating a Slack API token   14
        Connecting a bot   16
        Joining a channel   17
        Sending a message to a channel   18
        The slack object   18
        Getting all the channels   19
        Getting all members in a channel   21
        Sending a message to a channel   23
    Basic responses   25
        The authenticated event   25
        Using the message event   25
        Avoiding spam   27
    Sending a direct message   30
    Restricting access   31
        Adding and removing admins   33
    Debugging a bot   33
    Summary   37

Chapter 3: Adding Complexity	**39**
Responding to keywords	**39**
Using classes	39
Reactive bots	43
Bot commands	**46**
Sanitizing inputs	49
External API integration	**52**
Error handling	61
Summary	**62**
Chapter 4: Using Data	**63**
Introduction to Redis	**63**
Installing Redis	64
Mac OS X	65
Windows	65
Unix	65
Connecting to Redis	**66**
Saving and retrieving data	**68**
Connecting bots	69
Dynamic storage	70
Hashes, lists, and sets	72
Hashes	73
Lists	75
Sets	75
Sorted sets	76
Best practices	**77**
Simple to-do example	**82**
Summary	**88**
Chapter 5: Understanding and Responding to Natural Language	**89**
A brief introduction to natural language	**89**
Fundamentals of NLP	**91**
Tokenizers	**92**
Stemmers	**94**
String distance	**97**
Inflection	**99**
Displaying data in a natural way	**100**
When to use NLP?	**103**
Mentions	**105**
Classifiers	**108**
Using trained classifiers	**109**
Natural language generation	**115**

When should we use natural language generation?   **116**
The uncanny valley   **116**
Summary   **118**

Chapter 6: Webhooks and Slash Commands   **119**
  Webhooks   **120**
    Incoming webhooks   120
    Outgoing webhooks   125
  Slash commands   **129**
  In-channel and ephemeral responses   **138**
  Using webhooks and slash commands   **142**
  Summary   **143**

Chapter 7: Publishing Your App   **145**
    The Slack app directory   145
    Registering your app and obtaining tokens   147
    Understanding the OAuth process   149
    Scopes   156
    Submitting your app to the app directory   158
    Monetizing your bot   159
  Summary   **160**
    Further reading   161

Index   **163**

Preface

Chat bots have become big talking points in the world of business and software development. On the forefront of team communications is Slack, a platform for talking to colleagues and friends about absolutely anything. The engineers at Slack saw the potential and have designed a system that allows anyone to build their own Slack bots for productivity, ease of use, or just plain entertainment.

This book will teach you how to use a myriad of tools to build the very best bots for the Slack platform. Whether you are a programming beginner or a seasoned veteran, by the end of this book, you will be able to create high-quality bots whose only limit is the your imagination. You might also pick up a few tricks along the way.

What this book covers

Chapter 1, Getting Started with Slack, shows you what is Slack and why we should care about Slack bots.

Chapter 2, Your First Bot, takes you through building your first bot and explains how it works.

Chapter 3, Adding Complexity, helps us expand our first bot with new and useful functionalities.

Chapter 4, Using Data, teaches you how to use persistent data with your Slack bots.

Chapter 5, Understanding and Responding to Natural Language, teaches you about natural language processing and how to develop a bot that can comprehend and respond in natural language.

Chapter 6, Webhooks and Slash Commands, takes us through the uses of webhooks and Slash commands in a Slack setting.

Chapter 7, Publishing Your App, teaches you how to publish your app or bot so that it can be used by others outside your company.

What you need for this book

You should have an intermediate understanding of JavaScript and programming concepts in general. For this book, we will be using Node.js version 5.0.0. This means that the JavaScript code samples contained within will use ECMAScript 2015 (ES2015, more commonly known as ES6) features, which have been enabled in Node v5.0.0. For a full list of ES6 features enabled in Node.js version 5 and up, visit the Node.js website (https://nodejs.org/en/docs/es6/).

This book, its techniques, and the code samples within are OS-agnostic, although for debugging purposes, either the Google Chrome or Opera browser is required.

Who this book is for

This is a book for software developers who want to build Slack bots for their own company's use or for customers.

Conventions

In this book, you will find a number of text styles that distinguish between different kinds of information. Here are some examples of these styles and an explanation of their meaning.

Code words in text, database table names, folder names, filenames, file extensions, pathnames, dummy URLs, user input, and Twitter handles are shown as follows: "Save the file and then run the code via `iron-node` in your terminal."

A block of code is set as follows:

```
if (user && user.is_bot) {
  return;
}
```

When we wish to draw your attention to a particular part of a code block, the relevant lines or items are set in bold:

```
if (user && user.is_bot) {
  return;
}
```

Any command-line input or output is written as follows:

```
npm install -g iron-node
```

New terms and important words are shown in bold. Words that you see on the screen, for example, in menus or dialog boxes, appear in the text like this: "Either click on the **Step over** button in the top-right corner, symbolized by an arrow curving around a dot, or hit *F10* to step over to the next line."

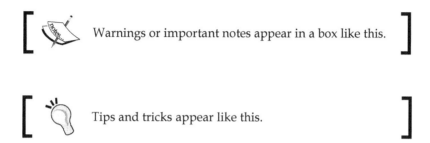

Warnings or important notes appear in a box like this.

Tips and tricks appear like this.

Reader feedback

Feedback from our readers is always welcome. Let us know what you think about this book — what you liked or disliked. Reader feedback is important for us as it helps us develop titles that you will really get the most out of.

To send us general feedback, simply e-mail feedback@packtpub.com, and mention the book's title in the subject of your message.

If there is a topic that you have expertise in and you are interested in either writing or contributing to a book, see our author guide at www.packtpub.com/authors.

Customer support

Now that you are the proud owner of a Packt book, we have a number of things to help you to get the most from your purchase.

Downloading the example code

You can download the example code files for this book from your account at http://www.packtpub.com. If you purchased this book elsewhere, you can visit http://www.packtpub.com/support and register to have the files e-mailed directly to you.

You can download the code files by following these steps:

1. Log in or register to our website using your e-mail address and password.
2. Hover the mouse pointer on the **SUPPORT** tab at the top.
3. Click on **Code Downloads & Errata**.
4. Enter the name of the book in the **Search** box.
5. Select the book for which you're looking to download the code files.
6. Choose from the drop-down menu where you purchased this book from.
7. Click on **Code Download**.

You can also download the code files by clicking on the **Code Files** button on the book's webpage at the Packt Publishing website. This page can be accessed by entering the book's name in the **Search** box. Please note that you need to be logged in to your Packt account.

Once the file is downloaded, please make sure that you unzip or extract the folder using the latest version of:

- WinRAR / 7-Zip for Windows
- Zipeg / iZip / UnRarX for Mac
- 7-Zip / PeaZip for Linux

The code bundle for the book is also hosted on GitHub at `https://github.com/PacktPublishing/Building-Slack-Bots`. We also have other code bundles from our rich catalog of books and videos available at `https://github.com/PacktPublishing/`. Check them out!

Errata

Although we have taken every care to ensure the accuracy of our content, mistakes do happen. If you find a mistake in one of our books—maybe a mistake in the text or the code—we would be grateful if you could report this to us. By doing so, you can save other readers from frustration and help us improve subsequent versions of this book. If you find any errata, please report them by visiting `http://www.packtpub.com/submit-errata`, selecting your book, clicking on the **Errata Submission Form** link, and entering the details of your errata. Once your errata are verified, your submission will be accepted and the errata will be uploaded to our website or added to any list of existing errata under the Errata section of that title.

To view the previously submitted errata, go to `https://www.packtpub.com/books/content/support` and enter the name of the book in the search field. The required information will appear under the **Errata** section.

Piracy

Piracy of copyrighted material on the Internet is an ongoing problem across all media. At Packt, we take the protection of our copyright and licenses very seriously. If you come across any illegal copies of our works in any form on the Internet, please provide us with the location address or website name immediately so that we can pursue a remedy.

Please contact us at `copyright@packtpub.com` with a link to the suspected pirated material.

We appreciate your help in protecting our authors and our ability to bring you valuable content.

Questions

If you have a problem with any aspect of this book, you can contact us at `questions@packtpub.com`, and we will do our best to address the problem.

1
Getting Started with Slack

This book will enable a beginner to create their own Slack bot either for amusement or professional purposes.

The ultimate goal of this book is for you to think of Slack as a development platform with great potential, rather than simply a chat client. As Slack continues its meteoric rise in popularity in the developer community, the possibilities and opportunities contained in Slack apps will prove to be a valuable tool in any developer's toolbox.

In this chapter, we introduce you to Slack and its possibilities. We will cover:

- An introduction to Slack
- Slack as a platform
- The end goal

Introduction to Slack

Launched in August 2013, Slack started as an internal communication tool utilized by small teams but has been rapidly morphing into a versatile communications platform used by many parties, including the open source community and large businesses.

Slack is a real-time messaging application that specializes in team communication. In a crowded space of productivity applications, Slack sets itself apart by providing extensive integrations with popular third-party apps and provides users with the platform to build their own integrations.

As of the beginning of 2016, Slack is used by approximately 2 million users daily, and spread across 60,000 teams that send 800 million messages per month (`http://expandedramblings.com/index.php/slack-statistics/`). Some of the more well known companies who use Slack include Airbnb, LinkedIn, and The New York Times. This service has become so popular, largely thanks to its impressive uptime rate of over 99.9 percent. What sets Slack apart from competition such as HipChat or Skype for Business is the determination of the company to open its platform for third-party developers in the form of an **application program interface (API)**. To spur the growth of their service as a platform, in December 2015 Slack pledged to invest $80 million into software projects that use its technology (`http://fortune.com/2015/12/15/slack-app-investment-fund/`). Added to the more than $320 million raised in funding for the company, it's safe to say that Slack will continue to be a driving force in the team productivity space in the years to come.

Slack as a platform

What many users perhaps don't know about Slack is that underneath the messaging client, a highly extensible platform exists that can be used to create apps and business tools that can simplify the development cycle, perform complex tasks, or just be downright silly.

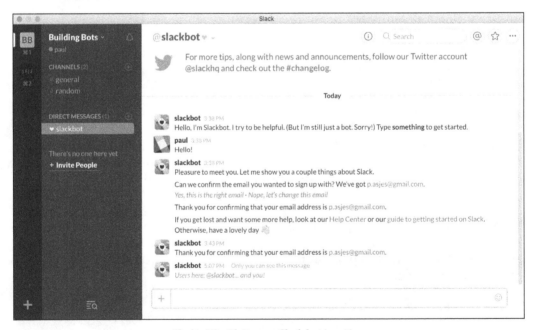

Slack's UI with its own Slack bot in action

This platform or API can be utilized to integrate third-party services into Slack's platform and leverage their extensive reach and user friendly interface. The said third-party applications can send data into Slack via incoming webhooks, execute actions outside of Slack with commands, or respond to commands as a bot user. The bot user or bot is the most interesting; they are so named as they can mimic human users by performing the same actions that any human can.

 Slack bots are software applications that run on the Slack **Real Time Messaging** (**RTM**) platform. Bots can be used to interact with external applications or your custom code in a conversational manner.

Some of the more popular bots include GitHub's multitasking Hubot (`https://hubot.github.com/`) and Meekan's scheduling bot (`http://meekan.com/slack/`), but many more of varying complexity are developed each day.

The most obvious and well known bot is Slack's own Slack bot, used for built-in Slack functions such as:

- Sending feedback to Slack
- Scheduling reminders
- Printing a list of all users in a channel

Another widely popular bot is Hubot. Originally developed by GitHub and ported to Slack by Slack themselves, Hubot can provide useful functionality such as GitHub activity tracking, which can keep you up to date with GitHub repositories.

 github BOT 14:20

[vendor-management-tool] New branch "paul/SOLS-1050-fix-print-job-create-bug" was pushed by PaulAsjes

[SolsCo/vendor-management-tool] Pull request submitted by PaulAsjes
#51 Fix Vendor Tools Dropping 1 Order Item During Print Job Creation

GitHub integration showing branch and pull request activity

You can also add infrastructure monitoring through Jenkins:

jenkins BOT 10:53
┃ (new PROD) Vendor Tools - #50 Started by user Paul Asjes (Open)

┃ (new PROD) Vendor Tools - #50 Starting... after 0.58 sec and counting (Open)

10:55 ☆ ┃ (new PROD) Vendor Tools - #50 Success after 1 min 24 sec (Open)

Jenkins integration bot showing build automation logs in Slack

Bots can transform Slack from a simple messaging client to an important business tool, benefitting any company that uses custom bots unique to their workflow. The beauty of the Slack platform is that anyone can create a functional bot in a few simple steps.

The end goal

Upon completing this book, the reader will be able to build a complex Slack bot that can perform the following tasks, amongst other things:

- Receive and send message sent in Slack
- Respond to user commands
- Process natural language
- Perform useful tasks on command (for example, fetch data from external sources)
- Insert custom data into Slack via webhooks and slash commands

Summary

This chapter gave you an overview on what Slack is, why it is noteworthy, and how its platform can be leveraged to create a myriad of useful apps. The next chapter will show you how to build your first simple Slack bot.

2
Your First Bot

Readers will be amazed at how few lines of code are required to get a basic bot up and running in their Slack environment. This chapter will walk the reader through the basics of building a Slack bot:

- Preparing your environment
- Creating a Slack API token
- Connecting your bot
- Joining a channel
- Sending a message to a channel
- Basic responses
- Sending a direct message
- Restricting access
- Debugging your bot

Although some of the concepts first outlined will be known to a more advanced reader, it is still recommended to read through the first few sections of this chapter to ensure that your environment is up and ready to go.

In this chapter, we will build a bot that performs the following actions:

- Connects to your Slack team
- Says hello to all the members of a channel after successfully connecting, distinguishing between real users and bot users
- Responds to users saying hello
- Sends a direct message to users who ask for the total amount of time the bot has been running (also known as uptime)
- Ensures that only administrative users can request the bot's uptime

Preparing your environment

Before we can get started with the first bot, the programming environment must be set up and configured to run Node.js applications and packages. Let's start at the very beginning with Node.

In brief, Node.js (also referred to as Node) is a JavaScript runtime built on Chrome's v8 JavaScript Engine. In practice, this means that JavaScript can be run outside of the usual browser environment, making JavaScript both a frontend and backend language.

Google Chrome's v8 JavaScript engine ensures that your JavaScript code runs fast and efficiently. Unlike in the world of browsers (and excepting Node versions), Node is maintained by a single open source foundation with hundreds of volunteer developers. This makes developing for Node much simpler than for browsers as you will not run into problems with varying JavaScript implementations across platforms.

In this book, we will be using major Version 5 (any version starting with 5) of Node. This allows us to use the newly implemented features of ECMAScript 2015 (better known as **ES2015** or **ES6**). Whenever an ES6 feature is used in this book for the first time, look for the accompanying code comment for a brief explanation on the feature.

Although many are implemented, not all ES6 features are currently available in Node and some are only available in **strict** mode. For more information, please visit the Node ES6 guide: `https://nodejs.org/en/docs/es6/`.

This section will briefly explain how to install Node.js and the Slack API on your development machine.

Installing Node.js

To install Node.js, head to the official Node website, `https://nodejs.org/`, download a v5 version and follow the onscreen instructions.

To test whether the installation succeeded, open up a terminal, type the following, and then hit *Enter*:

```
node
```

If node installed correctly, you should be able to type JavaScript commands and see the result:

Hello World in Node.js

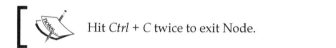 Hit *Ctrl + C* twice to exit Node.

Installing the development tools using NPM

Node Package Manager (**NPM**) is Node.js' package ecosystem and the tool used to install Node packages. As of the time of writing, there are more than 240,000 NPM packages available for download, with more being added every day.

Fortunately, NPM is automatically installed once the Node installation is complete. Let's start by installing a useful Node development tool called nodemon (http://nodemon.io/). Run the following in your terminal or command prompt:

```
npm install -g nodemon
```

This command will install the nodemon package globally (note the -g flag), meaning it can be run from any location on your computer. After the install command, you must specify the package you wish to install and can optionally select some flags that configure how the package is installed. Later on, we'll explore flags such as --save and --save-dev and their uses.

nodemon is a Node utility that will monitor any changes in your code and automatically restart your Node process. For our purposes, this will save us from having to stop the Node process and restart it every time we make a change to our code.

To demonstrate nodemon, let's look at an example. In your code editor of choice, paste the following and save it as hello-world.js:

```
console.log('Hello World!');
```

In your terminal, run the following:

```
nodemon hello-world.js
```

Your output should look like this:

```
[nodemon] 1.8.1
[nodemon] to restart at any time, enter `rs`
[nodemon] watching: *.*
[nodemon] starting `node hello-world.js`
Hello World!
[nodemon] clean exit - waiting for changes before restart
```

The same Hello World as before but using nodemon

Note how the console command ran and then the program exited. `nodemon` then enters "watch mode", where it will wait for any files (indicated by the `*.*` wildcard) to change and then subsequently restart the Node process. `nodemon` can be further customized to watch or ignore specific files. Visit the website `http://nodemon.io/` for more information.

To manually restart the Node process without changing a file that `nodemon` watches, type *rs* followed by the *Enter* key.

Creating a new project

Now that the basics of Node and NPM are covered, we will look at creating a new Node project and expanding our knowledge of NPM.

A Node project can contain dependencies and development dependencies. The former are segments of code (or packages) that are required to run the project whereas the latter are segments of code used solely for development. In our previous example, `nodemon` would be considered a development dependency, as it would not be used in a production environment.

The dependencies of a Node project are stored in a **JavaScript Object Notation (JSON)** file named `package.json`. The JSON file contains information about the Node project, including a list of dependencies, the versions of the dependencies, and information about the package author(s). This allows easy installation of a project via NPM.

Let's create one of our own. Open up a terminal window and create a new folder by typing in the following and hitting *Enter*:

```
mkdir helloWorld && cd helloWorld
```

This creates a new directory and navigates to said directory. Next, enter the following:

```
npm init
```

Follow the onscreen prompts and you will end up with something like this:

```
paul@Batmac   ~/helloWorld    npm init
This utility will walk you through creating a package.json file.
It only covers the most common items, and tries to guess sensible defaults.

See `npm help json` for definitive documentation on these fields
and exactly what they do.

Use `npm install <pkg> --save` afterwards to install a package and
save it as a dependency in the package.json file.

Press ^C at any time to quit.
name: (helloWorld) helloworld
version: (1.0.0)
description: My first Slack bot!
entry point: (index.js)
test command:
git repository:
keywords:
author: Paul Asjes
license: (ISC)
About to write to /Users/paul/helloWorld/package.json:

{
  "name": "helloworld",
  "version": "1.0.0",
  "description": "My first Slack bot!",
  "main": "index.js",
  "scripts": {
    "test": "echo \"Error: no test specified\" && exit 1"
  },
  "author": "Paul Asjes",
  "license": "ISC"
}


Is this ok? (yes) yes
```

Example of NPM init running successfully

Once completed, you'll find that a package.json file has been created in your directory; see the preceding screenshot for an example of what that JSON file contains.

Now that we've created a template for our app, let's create an entry point JavaScript file and install some dependencies:

```
touch index.js
npm install @slack/client --save
```

These commands create an empty JavaScript file named index and install the Slack **Real Time Messaging (RTM)** client. Note how @slack/client now appears under dependencies in package.json. This is due to the --save flag used in the last command. The save flag indicates that this NPM package is required to run this app.

As of Version 2, the Slack client API has moved to using NPM organizations. Indicated by the @ character in the package name, this means that Slack (the company) can publish packages under the umbrella organization of @slack. Other than the additional character, the package does not differ from other, non-organization packages.

Should you wish to distribute your bot and allow others to work on or with it, you can easily install all required packages as dictated in package.json by running npm install in the project's directory.

Alternatively to the save flag, you can specify that a package is only required for development by using the --save-dev flag. This will add the package to the devDependencies section in package.json. This allows us to specify that this package only needs to be installed if the user intends to do some development.

This is particularly useful for servers running your code, where you would want to omit development packages altogether.

Your package.json file should now look something like this:

```
{
  "name": "helloworld",
  "version": "1.0.0",
  "description": "My first Slack bot!",
  "main": "index.js",
  "scripts": {
    "test": "echo \"Error: no test specified\" && exit 1"
  },
```

```
    "author": "Paul Asjes",
    "license": "ISC",
    "dependencies": {
      "@slack/client": "^2.0.6",
    }
}
```

Now that the Slack client is listed as a dependency, it will be automatically installed when the following command is run from within this directory:

`npm install`

You can test this by deleting the `node_modules` folder and then running the preceding command:

```
helloworld@1.0.0 /Users/paul/helloWorld
└─┬ slack-client@1.5.1
  ├── coffee-script@1.9.3
  ├─┬ https-proxy-agent@1.0.0
  │ ├─┬ agent-base@2.0.1
  │ │ └── semver@5.0.3
  │ ├─┬ debug@2.2.0
  │ │ └── ms@0.7.1
  │ └── extend@3.0.0
  ├── log@1.4.0
  └─┬ ws@0.8.1
    ├─┬ bufferutil@1.2.1
    │ ├── bindings@1.2.1
    │ └── nan@2.2.0
    ├── options@0.0.6
    ├── ultron@1.0.2
    └── utf-8-validate@1.2.1
```

All our dependencies are installed

Note how the `slack-client` package has its own dependencies, which were automatically installed into the `node_modules` folder.

Now, we will add some code to our entry point JavaScript file. Open up `index.js` and enter the following code:

```javascript
// Enable strict mode, this allows us to use ES6 specific syntax
// such as 'const' and 'let'
'use strict';

// Import the Real Time Messaging (RTM) client
// from the Slack API in node_modules
const RtmClient = require('@slack/client').RtmClient;

// The memory data store is a collection of useful functions we
// can
// include in our RtmClient
const MemoryDataStore = require('@slack/client').MemoryDataStore;

// Import the RTM event constants from the Slack API
const RTM_EVENTS = require('@slack/client').RTM_EVENTS;

// Import the client event constants from the Slack API
const CLIENT_EVENTS = require('@slack/client').CLIENT_EVENTS;

const token = '';

// The Slack constructor takes 2 arguments:
// token - String representation of the Slack token
// opts - Objects with options for our implementation
let slack = new RtmClient(token, {
  // Sets the level of logging we require
  logLevel: 'debug',
  // Initialize a data store for our client, this will
  // load additional helper functions for the storing
  // and retrieval of data
  dataStore: new MemoryDataStore(),
  // Boolean indicating whether Slack should automatically
  // reconnect after an error response
  autoReconnect: true,
  // Boolean indicating whether each message should be marked as
  // read
  // or not after it is processed
  autoMark: true
});

// Add an event listener for the RTM_CONNECTION_OPENED
// event, which is called
```

```
  // when the bot connects to a channel. The Slack API can
  // subscribe to events by using the 'on' method
  slack.on(CLIENT_EVENTS.RTM.RTM_CONNECTION_OPENED, () => {
    // Get the user's name
    let user = slack.dataStore.getUserById(slack.activeUserId);

    // Get the team's name
    let team = slack.dataStore.getTeamById(slack.activeTeamId);

    // Log the slack team name and the bot's name, using ES6's
    // template
    // string syntax
    console.log(`Connected to ${team.name} as ${user.name}`);
  });

  // Start the login process
  slack.start();
```

Save the file and run the program by executing the following command:

`node index.js`

You should immediately notice that something is wrong:

```
verbose: attempting to connect via the RTM API
debug: { '0': 'connecting' }
debug: { '0': 'unable_to_rtm_start', '1': 'not_authed' }
error: unrecoverable failure connecting to the RTM API: not_authed
debug: { '0': 'disconnect',
  '1': 'unrecoverable failure connecting to the RTM API',
  '2': 'not_authed' }
```

Debug and error logs are shown

Notice how the built-in logger outputs both debug and error messages. The error indicates that Slack cannot connect due to an authentication error. This is because we have not provided a Slack API token. The access token is a unique ID generated for your bot. By using it, you enable your bot to authenticate with Slack's servers and interact with the Slack client.

In our example, the token is set to an empty string, which will not work. Let's then retrieve an access token from Slack.

Detailed steps to download the code bundle are mentioned in the *Preface* of this book. Please have a look.

The code bundle for the book is also hosted on GitHub at `https://github.com/PacktPublishing/Building-Slack-Bots`. We also have other code bundles from our rich catalog of books and videos available at `https://github.com/PacktPublishing/`. Check them out!

Creating a Slack API token

Open up a browser and navigate to `https://my.slack.com/apps/build/custom-integration`.

Follow these steps:

1. Select **Bots** from the list of available custom integrations.

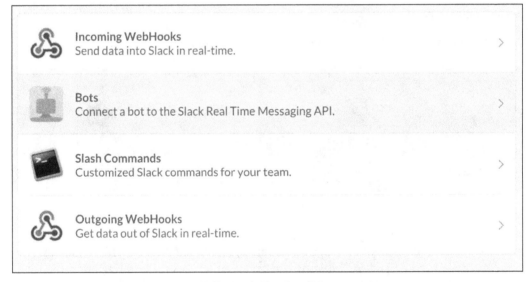

Custom integrations list

2. Select a name and click on **Add Bot Integration**. The name of your bot can be changed later, so don't worry about picking a well thought-out name immediately.

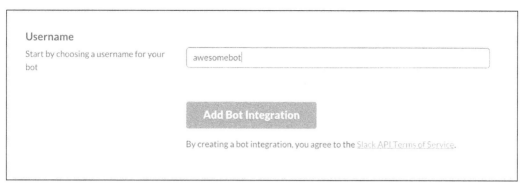

Adding a bot integration

3. Copy down the newly generated API token. As an optional step, you can choose to customize the bot further in this screen.

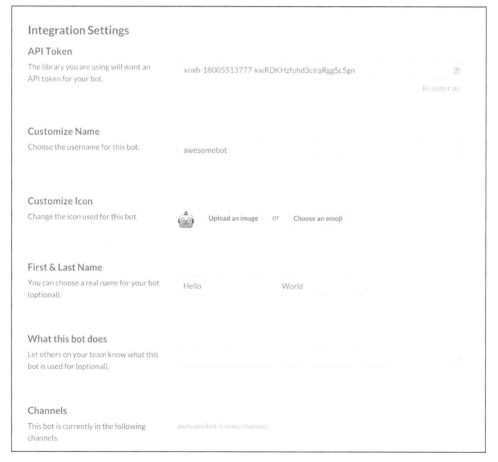

Optional settings for your bot

> Although optional, it is recommended to choose an icon for your bot. For this example, we will use the `robot_face` emoji; however, a good bot should have an icon that represents the purpose of the bot.

Although you can give bots duplicate first and last names, the bot's username must be unique to your team. Providing a first name, last name, and description is optional but advisable as it provides information at a glance on what your bot does.

4. Click on **Save Integration** at the bottom of the page.

> If you wish to remove or disable this bot at a later stage, you can do that from this same page.

Connecting a bot

Now that we've generated an API token, replace the empty string assigned to `token` in `index.js` and run the program again.

> Now is a good time to use `nodemon` rather than `node` to ensure automatic restarts when code is changed.

You will probably see a whole page of debug information show up. While useful, this can also hinder our progress as our own console logs might be difficult to spot. Instead of playing hide and seek, let's first change our logging settings in the client.

Switch this line:

```
logLevel: 'debug',
```

Use the following line:

```
logLevel: 'error',
```

This will instruct the client to only output error messages when the program crashes or a syntax error occurs.

Restart the program (or just save the file and let nodemon do the work):

```
[Thu Jan 07 2016 20:56:07 GMT-0500 (EST)] INFO Connecting...
Connected to Building Bots as awesomebot
```

If you see something similar to the preceding output in your terminal, congratulations! Your first bot is successfully connected to Slack! You will now see your bot in the **Direct Messages** section of your Slack client; click on the bot's name to open a private direct message.

 Throughout this book, you will encounter the title Building Bots. This is simply the title of the Slack team the author used and will be different from your own.

 Hello World ● @awesomebot

This is the very beginning of your direct message history with **awesomebot**. Direct messages are private between the two of you. Sharing a private file here will not make it public, but it will allow **awesomebot** to see and share it.

Today

 paul 21:18
Hi bot!

A direct message (DM) with your bot

Your bot is alive and well. However, it is fairly limited in its abilities. We will remedy that shortly, but first let's ensure that the bot can interact with a wider audience.

Joining a channel

Bots cannot join channels programmatically; this is a design choice as bots should not be allowed to enter private channels without being invited. When a bot joins a channel, all the channel's activity can be monitored by the bot. A bot could potentially save all channel messages, a potentially nefarious activity that shouldn't be allowed to happen automatically.

For a complete list of what actions bots can and cannot perform, see the Slack bot user documentation at `https://api.slack.com/bot-users`.

Bots are restricted in the actions they can perform themselves. As such, bots need to be invited to channels via the `invite` command within the Slack client:

`/invite [BOT_NAME]`

After this, you'll get confirmation of the bot entering the channel like this:

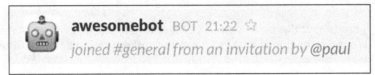

awesomebot BOT 21:22 ☆

joined #general from an invitation by @paul

The bot enters the world

Note that when a bot joins a channel, it remains there even if the bot's Node process is stopped. It shows the same characteristics as an offline user. This ensures that invitation needs only to happen once per bot and per channel.

To remove a bot from a channel, use the remove command within the Slack client:

`/remove [BOT_NAME]`

 Although all users can invite into a channel, only admins can actively remove users and bots from channels.

To make testing easier and to not disrupt other users in your team, it is a good idea to create a bot testing channel and invite your bot. For the purposes of this book, the testing channel is named `bot-test`.

Sending a message to a channel

We now have a connected bot, but it admittedly is a rather useless one. Let's remedy that by getting our bot to say "Hello" to every channel that it resides in.

The slack object

You might have noticed the following on line 18 in the preceding code example:

```
let user = slack.dataStore.getUserById(slack.activeUserId);
```

Here, we see that the `slack` object contains a myriad of information about the bot's current environment. Let's explore the data contained within. Replace line 18 with this modified `console.log` method:

```
console.log(slack);
```

You should see a large object printed out in your terminal. While we won't go through all the values, here are some of interest:

Name	Type	Function
`activeUserId`	String	The internal user ID. This can be used to get more information about the current user.
`activeUserId`	String	The internal team ID. Again, it can be used to get more information about the team.
`dataStore`	Object	If a data store is initialized, this object contains a myriad of information stored within the Slack API.
`channels` (child of `dataStore`)	Object	Contains a list of all the channels available in this team.
`channel` (child of channels)	Object	Contains further info on the channel. Whether the user requesting this information is a member or not is available through the `is_member` property
`dms` (child of `dataStore`)	Object	A list of all the direct message channels this user is a part of. Note: even if no messages were ever sent the direct message channel is still considered open.
`users` (child of `dataStore`)	Object	A list of all users in this team.

Getting all the channels

You'll note from the preceding table that the `channels` object returns all the channels in this team. For our purposes, we only want the channels in which our bot resides. To achieve this, we can loop through the `channels` object and return exactly what we need. Add the following to the end of `index.js`:

```
// Returns an array of all the channels the bot resides in
function getChannels(allChannels) {
  let channels = [];

  // Loop over all channels
  for (let id in allChannels) {
```

```
    // Get an individual channel
    let channel = allChannels[id];

    // Is this user a member of the channel?
    if (channel.is_member) {
      // If so, push it to the array
      channels.push(channel);
    }
  }

  return channels;
}
```

Now, replace the Slack open event listener with this:

```
// Add an event listener for the RTM_CONNECTION_OPENED event,
//  which is called when the bot
// connects to a channel. The Slack API can subscribe to
// events by using the 'on' method
slack.on(CLIENT_EVENTS.RTM.RTM_CONNECTION_OPENED, () => {
  // Get the user's name
  let user = slack.dataStore.getUserById(slack.activeUserId);

  // Get the team's name
  let team = slack.dataStore.getTeamById(slack.activeTeamId);

  // Log the slack team name and the bot's name, using ES6's
  // template string syntax
  console.log(`Connected to ${team.name} as ${user.name}`);

  // Note how the dataStore object contains a list of all
  // channels available
  let channels = getChannels(slack.dataStore.channels);

  // Use Array.map to loop over every instance and return an
  // array of the names of each channel. Then chain Array.join
  // to convert the names array to a string
  let channelNames = channels.map((channel) => {
    return channel.name;
  }).join(', ');

  console.log(`Currently in: ${channelNames}`)
});
```

Switch to your terminal and you should see the following output:

```
[Sun Jan 10 2016 15:35:53 GMT-0500 (EST)] INFO Connecting...
Connected to Building Bots as awesomebot
Currently in: bot-test
```

Listing the channels the bot resides in

Now that your bot knows which channels it's in, it can start to send messages. We'll start with the bot sending a simple "Hello" message to everyone in the channel.

Getting all members in a channel

We have the channel object, so getting the members within is easy. Add this to the RTM_CONNECTION_OPENED event listener:

```
// log the members of the channel
channels.forEach((channel) => {
  console.log('Members of this channel: ', channel.members);
});
```

This is the result:

```
[Sun Jan 10 2016 15:43:16 GMT-0500 (EST)] INFO Connecting...
Connected to Building Bots as awesomebot
Currently in: bot-test
Members of this channel:  [ 'U0HKKH1TR', 'U0J05F3NV' ]
```

A list of user IDs

Well that wasn't quite what we expected, perhaps. The Slack API has returned a list of user IDs rather than an array of member objects. This makes sense as a large channel containing several hundred users would result in an unwieldy and large array of member objects. Not to worry, the Slack API provides us with the tools we need to get more information by using these user IDs. Replace the previous snippet with this and then save the file:

```
// log the members of the channel
channels.forEach((channel) => {
  // get the members by ID using the data store's
  //'getUserByID' function
  let members = channel.members.map((id) => {
    return slack.dataStore.getUserById(id);
  });
```

```
// Each member object has a 'name' property, so let's
// get an array of names and join them via Array.join
let memberNames = members.map((member) => {
  return member.name;
}).join(', ');

console.log('Members of this channel: ', memberNames);
});
```

The output for this code can be seen in the following screenshot:

```
[Sun Jan 10 2016 15:35:53 GMT-0500 (EST)] INFO Connecting...
Connected to Building Bots as awesomebot
Currently in: bot-test
Members of this channel:  paul, awesomebot
```

The users of the channel using their usernames

Notice how the bot is also listed in the channel members list. Our current goal is to say hello to everyone in the channel; however, we should try to avoid having the bot talking to itself.

We can use the is_bot property on the member object to determine whether a user is a bot:

```
// log the members of the channel
channels.forEach((channel) => {
  // get the members by ID using the data store's
  // 'getUserByID' function
  let members = channel.members.map((id) => {
    return slack.dataStore.getUserById(id);
  });

  // Filter out the bots from the member list using Array.filter
  members = members.filter((member) => {
    return !member.is_bot;
  });

  // Each member object has a 'name' property, so let's
  // get an array of names and join them via Array.join
  let memberNames = members.map((member) => {
    return member.name;
  }).join(', ');

  console.log('Members of this channel: ', memberNames);
});
```

```
[Sun Jan 10 2016 15:51:29 GMT-0500 (EST)] INFO Connecting...
Connected to Building Bots as awesomebot
Currently in: bot-test
Members of this channel:  paul
```

The users of the channel, without bots

Wonderful! Now that we are done with this, the next step is to send a message to the channel.

Sending a message to a channel

The channel object contains all the tools required for bot communication. In the following code, we will build upon the previous code snippets and send a "Hello" message addressing each person in the channel once the bot connects. All of these actions will happen in the open event listener. Here it is in its entirety:

```
// Add an event listener for the RTM_CONNECTION_OPENED event,
// which is called when the bot connects to a channel. The Slack API
// can subscribe to events by using the 'on' method
slack.on(CLIENT_EVENTS.RTM.RTM_CONNECTION_OPENED, () => {
  // Get the user's name
  let user = slack.dataStore.getUserById(slack.activeUserId);

  // Get the team's name
  let team = slack.dataStore.getTeamById(slack.activeTeamId);

  // Log the slack team name and the bot's name, using ES6's
  // template string syntax
  console.log(`Connected to ${team.name} as ${user.name}`);

  // Note how the dataStore object contains a list of all
  // channels available
  let channels = getChannels(slack.dataStore.channels);

  // Use Array.map to loop over every instance and return an
  // array of the names of each channel. Then chain Array.join
  // to convert the names array to a string
  let channelNames = channels.map((channel) => {
    return channel.name;
  }).join(', ');

  console.log(`Currently in: ${channelNames}`)
```

```
    // log the members of the channel
  channels.forEach((channel) => {
    // get the members by ID using the data store's
    // 'getUserByID' function
    let members = channel.members.map((id) => {
      return slack.dataStore.getUserById(id);
    });

    // Filter out the bots from the member list using Array.filter
    members = members.filter((member) => {
      return !member.is_bot;
    });

    // Each member object has a 'name' property, so let's
    // get an array of names and join them via Array.join
    let memberNames = members.map((member) => {
      return member.name;
    }).join(', ');

    console.log('Members of this channel: ', memberNames);

    // Send a greeting to everyone in the channel
    slack.sendMessage(`Hello ${memberNames}!`, channel.id);
  });
});
```

As soon as you run the code, you should be greeted by a notification from the Slack client that you have been mentioned in a message, as shown in the following screenshot:

Our bot speaks its first words

Let's ramp up our bot's complexity by giving it the ability to respond to messages.

Basic responses

The Slack API can be configured to execute methods once certain events are dispatched, as seen earlier with the RTM_CONNECTION_OPENED event. Now, we will dive into other useful events provided to us.

The authenticated event

So far, we have seen how to add functionality to Slack's RTM_CONNECTION_OPENED event triggered by the bot entering a channel and an error occurring, respectively. If you wish to execute some code when a bot logs in but before it connects to a channel, you can use the AUTHENTICATED event:

```
slack.on(CLIENT_EVENTS.RTM.AUTHENTICATED, (rtmStartData) => {
  console.log(`Logged in as ${rtmStartData.self.name} of team
  ${rtmStartData.team.name}, but not yet connected to a channel`);
});
```

This gives the following output:

```
[Mon Jan 18 2016 21:37:24 GMT-0500 (EST)] INFO Connecting...
Logged in as awesomebot of team Building Bots, but not yet connected to a
channel
```

Now, we will introduce the *message* event.

Using the message event

The message event will trigger every time a message is sent to a channel the bot is in or in a direct message to the bot. The message object contains useful data such as the originating user, the originating channel, and the timestamp it was sent.

Paste the following into index.js and then send the message "Hello bot!" to a channel that your bot is a member of:

```
slack.on(RTM_EVENTS.MESSAGE, (message) => {
  let user = slack.dataStore.getUserById(message.user)

  if (user && user.is_bot) {
    return;
  }
```

```
    let channel = slack.dataStore.
    getChannelGroupOrDMById(message.channel);

if (message.text) {
  let msg = message.text.toLowerCase();

  if (/(hello|hi) (bot|awesomebot)/g.test(msg)) {
    slack.sendMessage(`Hello to you too, ${user.name}!`,
    channel.id);
  }
}
});
```

This should result in something like this:

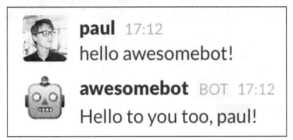

A more personal greeting from the bot

Let's look at the code again in detail, starting from the top:

```
slack.on(RTM_EVENTS.MESSAGE, (message) => {
  let user = slack.dataStore.getUserById(message.user)

  if (user && user.is_bot) {
    return;
  }
}
```

This should be familiar, as it's similar to what we've used before, except we're now using the MESSAGE event from the RTM_EVENTS object. We also make sure the message sender isn't a bot:

```
    let channel = slack.dataStore.
    getChannelGroupOrDMById(message.channel);
```

The `getChannelGroupOrDMById` method lets us grab the channel for every message sent. This is particularly useful if our bot happens to inhabit multiple channels. The code is as follows:

```
if (message.text) {
  let msg = message.text.toLowerCase();

  if (/(hello|hi) (bot|awesomebot)/g.test(msg)) {
    slack.sendMessage(`Hello to you too, ${user.name}!`,
    channel.id);
      }
}
```

A message does not necessarily contain text; it is also possible that the message is a file, an image, or even an emoji. Therefore, we have to do a little type checking to make sure the message received is indeed text based. Once the text type is confirmed, we use a regular expression to test whether the message received contains certain keywords in a specific order. The `RegExp.test` method will return true when the message received contains the words "Hello" or "Hi" followed by either "bot" or "awesomebot." If true, a response is sent back to the channel using the familiar `slack.sendMessage` method.

> When evaluating incoming text, it is almost always a good idea to first convert the body of the text message to lowercase in order to avoid case sensitive errors.

Avoiding spam

Infinite loops happen occasionally when developing; it is entirely possible that you accidentally program a bot to send a message in an infinite loop, flooding the channel with spam. Observe the following code:

```
if (/(hello|hi) (bot|awesomebot)/g.test(msg)) {
  // Infinite loop spamming the channel every 100 milliseconds
  setInterval(() => {
    slack.sendMessage('Spam!', channel.id);
  }, 100);
}
```

Take a look at the screenshot of the result:

A bot spamming the channel

In the terminal or command prompt, you should see this:

```
Error: { code: -1, msg: 'slow down, too many messages...' }
Error: { code: -1, msg: 'slow down, too many messages...' }
Error: { code: -1, msg: 'slow down, too many messages...' }
Error: { code: -1, msg: 'slow down, too many messages...' }
Error: { code: -1, msg: 'slow down, too many messages...' }
Error: { code: -1, msg: 'slow down, too many messages...' }
```

The Slack API deals with the spam

Luckily, the Slack API has a built in guard against such unfortunate events. If 20 messages are sent by a single user in a very short time frame, the Slack server will refuse to post more messages and return an error. This has the added effect of causing our bot to get stuck and eventually crash.

The Slack platform will guard against spam attacks flooding the channel; however, it is likely that the offending bot will crash.

To prevent this from happening, it is highly advisable to *never* place a `slack.sendMessage` method call within a loop or within a `setInterval` method.

Channels with many users and thus high volume could potentially lead to accidentally triggering the "slow down" response from the Slack platform. To prevent this, keep track of the time difference between messages:

```
if (/(hello|hi) (bot|awesomebot)/g.test(msg)) {
  // Get the timestamp when the above message was sent
  let sentTime = Date.now();

  setInterval(() => {
    // Get the current timestamp
    let currentTime = Date.now();

    // Make sure we only allow a message once a full second has
    // passed
    if ((currentTime - sentTime) > 1000) {

      slack.sendMesssage('Limiting my messages to 1 per second',
      channel.id);

      // Set the new sentTime
      sentTime = Date.now();
    }
  }, 100);
}
```

 paul 18:33
hello bot

 awesomebot BOT 18:33
Hello to you too, paul!

Limiting my messages to 1 per second

Limiting my messages to 1 per second

Limiting my messages to 1 per second

Limiting my messages to 1 per second

Limiting the bot's messages

Every time the `setInterval` function is called, we generate a new timestamp called `currentTime`. By comparing `currentTime` to the timestamp of the message (defined as `sentTime`), we can artificially limit the messages being sent on the bot side by making sure the difference between the two is more than 1,000 milliseconds in length.

The Slack API provides a timestamp on the channel object accessible via `channel.latest.ts`; this provides a timestamp for the latest message received in the channel. While still useful, it is recommended to use local timestamps instead, as the Slack API provides information on the latest message received rather than the latest message sent by the bot.

Sending a direct message

A **direct message (DM)** channel is a channel that only operates between two users. By design, it cannot have more or less than two users and is meant for private communication. Sending a DM is remarkably similar to sending a message to a channel, as the `dm` object is almost identical to the `channel` object.

Consider the following snippet:

```
slack.on(RTM_EVENTS.MESSAGE, (message) => {
  let user = slack.dataStore.getUserById(message.user)

  if (user && user.is_bot) {
    return;
  }

  let channel = slack.dataStore.
  getChannelGroupOrDMById(message.channel);

  if (message.text) {
    let msg = message.text.toLowerCase();

    if (/uptime/g.test(msg)) {
      let dm = slack.dataStore.getDMByName(user.name);

      let uptime = process.uptime();

      // get the uptime in hours, minutes and seconds
      let minutes = parseInt(uptime / 60, 10),
          hours = parseInt(minutes / 60, 10),
```

```
        seconds = parseInt(uptime - (minutes * 60) - ((hours *
        60) * 60), 10);

        slack.sendMessage(`I have been running for: ${hours} hours,
        ${minutes} minutes and ${seconds} seconds.`, dm.id);
    }
});
```

In this example, our bot will send a DM with the current uptime to any user who uses the key phrase `uptime`:

paul 21:08
uptime

awesomebot BOT 21:08
I have been running for: 0 hours, 2 minutes and 27 seconds.

Uptime can be a very useful statistic

Note that the bot will send a DM to the user, regardless of which channel the command `uptime` is sent as long as the bot is around to hear the command as a member of that channel or DM. In the preceding image, the command was issued in the DM itself. This is because both channels and DMs subscribe to the `message` event; it is important to remember this when sending responses meant for channels rather than DMs and vice versa.

Restricting access

Occasionally, you might wish to restrict bot commands to administrators of your Slack team. A good example is a bot that controls a project's deploy process. This can be immensely powerful but perhaps not something that you want every user to have access to. Only administrators (also known as admins) should have the authority to access such functions. Admins are special users who have administrative powers over the Slack team. Luckily, restricting such access is easy with the `is_admin` property attached to a user object.

In the following example, we'll restrict the `uptime` command demonstrated in the previous topic to admin users, notifying the restricted user that they can't use that command:

```
slack.on(RTM_EVENTS.MESSAGE, (message) => {
    let user = slack.dataStore.getUserById(message.user)
```

```
if (user && user.is_bot) {
  return;
}

let channel = slack.dataStore.
getChannelGroupOrDMById(message.channel);

if (message.text) {
  let msg = message.text.toLowerCase();

  if (/uptime/g.test(msg)) {
    if (!user.is_admin) {
      slack.sendMessage(`Sorry ${user.name}, but that
      functionality is only for admins.`, channel.id);
      return;
    }

    let dm = slack.dataStore.getDMByName(user.name);

    let uptime = process.uptime();

    // get the uptime in hours, minutes and seconds
    let minutes = parseInt(uptime / 60, 10),
        hours = parseInt(minutes / 60, 10),
        seconds = parseInt(uptime - (minutes * 60) - ((hours *
        60) * 60), 10);

    slack.sendMessage(`I have been running for: ${hours} hours,
    ${minutes} minutes and ${seconds} seconds.`, dm.id);
  }
});
```

Now when non-admin users issue the uptime command, they will get the following message:

 joshua 21:20
uptime

 awesomebot BOT 21:20
Sorry joshua, but that functionality is only for admins.

Restricting the bot to admin users

The use of `user.is_admin` is to determine whether a user is an admin or not.

Adding and removing admins

To add or remove admins to your team, visit `https://my.slack.com/ admin#active` and click on a user.

Admins and owners have the ability to kick other members from channels and to delete messages that aren't their own. Although these are the default settings, they can be edited at `https://my.slack.com/admin/settings#channel_management_ restrictions`.

Bots cannot be admins or owners; for more information on team permissions, visit `https://get.slack.help/hc/en-us/articles/201314026-Understanding- roles-permissions-inside-Slack`.

Debugging a bot

It is inevitable that eventually you will encounter a bug in your bot that is difficult to squash. The worst are bugs that don't cause your program to crash and thus don't provide a useful stack trace and line number for where the crash happened. For most issues, the `console.log()` method will be enough to help you track down the bug, for the more tenacious bugs however we will need a true debugging environment. This section will introduce you to `iron-node` (`https://s-a.github.io/iron- node/`), a cross-platform JavaScript debugging environment based on Chrome's dev tools.

Start by installing `iron-node`:

```
npm install -g iron-node
```

Note again the use of the `-g` flag, which installs the application globally.

Before we can start debugging, we need to add a breakpoint to our code, which tells the debugger to stop the code and allow for deeper inspection. Add the `debugger` statement to our previous code, within the `slack.openDM()` code block:

```
if (/uptime/g.test(msg)) {
  debugger;

  if (!user.is_admin) {
```

```
    slack.sendMessage(`Sorry ${user.name}, but that functionality
    is only for admins.`, channel.id);
    return;
}

let dm = slack.dataStore.getDMByName(user.name);

let uptime = process.uptime();

// get the uptime in hours, minutes and seconds
let minutes = parseInt(uptime / 60, 10),
    hours = parseInt(minutes / 60, 10),
    seconds = parseInt(uptime - (minutes * 60) - ((hours * 60) *
    60), 10);

    slack.sendMessage(`I have been running for: ${hours} hours,
    ${minutes} minutes and ${seconds} seconds.`, dm.id);
}
```

Save the file and then run the code via `iron-node` in your terminal:

```
iron-node index.js
```

Immediately, you should see the `iron-node` interface pop up:

The iron-node interface

Chrome users will perhaps notice that this interface is exactly like Chrome's developer tools window. It is advisable to spend some time familiarizing yourself with this interface if you haven't used it before. Let's discuss some basic functionality to get you started.

You can switch to the console tab to see the node output, or you can also hit *Esc* to show the console at the bottom of the screen.

Our debugger was placed within a message event listener, so send a command to the bot (uptime in the last example) and watch what happens next.

Setting a breakpoint with the "debugger" statement

The bot's execution has been paused by the debugger, so you can inspect properties and determine the source of the bug.

Either click on the **Step over** button in the top-right corner, symbolized by an arrow curving around a dot, or hit *F10* to step over to the next line.

Use your mouse to hover over the different objects in this line of code to retrieve more information about them.

```
let dm = slack.getChannelGroupOrDMByID(data.channel.id);

// create a new Date object
let uptime = process.uptime();

// get the uptime in hours, minutes a    Object
let minutes = parseInt(uptime / 60, 1    already_open: true
    hours = parseInt(minutes / 60, 10    ▶ channel: Object
    seconds = parseInt(uptime - (minu    no_op: true
                                         ok: true
dm.send(`I have been running for: ${h    ▶ __proto__: Object
;



  the login process
gin();

ns an array of all the channels the b
 getChannels(allChannels) {
annels = [];
```

Inspecting a property in the paused program

Keep clicking on the **Step over** button to progress through the code, or click on the **Resume script execution** button to the left of the **Step over** button to allow the program to continue until it encounters another debugger breakpoint.

Not only can you inspect variables and properties while the bot is executing, but you can also edit their values, causing different outputs. Observe how we can edit the uptime variable in our code and set it to 1000:

```
// get the Node uptime in seconds
let uptime = process.uptime();   uptime = 40.064

// get the uptime in hours, minutes and seconds
let minutes = parseInt(uptime / 60, 10),    minutes = 0, uptime = 40.064
    hours = parseInt(minutes / 60, 10),    hours = 0
    seconds = parseInt(uptime - (minutes * 60) - ((hours * 60) * 60), 10);    seconds = 40, uptime = 40.064
```

uptime is set by the program to 40.064

In the console area, we can edit JavaScript variables whilst the program is running:

```
> uptime
< 40.064
> uptime = 1000;
< 1000
```

In the console, we check the value of uptime again, and then set it to a value of 1000. Now when we look back at the variables, we should see the updated values:

```
// get the uptime in hours, minutes and seconds
let minutes = parseInt(uptime / 60, 10),   minutes = 16, uptime = 1000
    hours = parseInt(minutes / 60, 10),   hours = 0
    seconds = parseInt(uptime - (minutes * 60) - ((hours * 60) * 60), 10);   seconds = 40, uptime = 1000
```

The new value of uptime is reflected in the next few lines

When we resume the program, our bot will send its message based on our updated variables:

 awesomebot BOT 16:43
I have been running for: 0 hours, 16 minutes and 40 seconds.

We continue the program and the bot sends the new values to the channel.

 For best debugging practices, either disable your bot's ability to send messages or invite your bot to a private channel to avoid spamming other users.

As `iron-node` is based on Chrome's developer tools, you can use the previous techniques interchangeably with Chrome.

To debug and fix memory issues, you can use the developer tools' profiler and heap snapshot tool. For more information on these topics, please visit the following links:

* `https://developers.google.com/web/tools/chrome-devtools/profile/rendering-tools/js-execution`
* `https://developers.google.com/web/tools/chrome-devtools/profile/memory-problems/?hl=en`

Summary

In this chapter, we saw how to install the prerequisite technologies, how to obtain a Slack token for a bot, and how to set up a new Slack bot project. As a result, you can reuse the lessons learned to easily scaffold a new bot project. You should now be able to program a bot that can send messages to channels, direct messages as well as craft basic responses. Finally, we discussed how to debug a Node.js-based bot using the `iron-node` debugger.

In the next chapter, we will see how to make our bot more complex by adding third-party API support and by programming our first bot command.

3
Adding Complexity

With the first bot done, it's time to learn how to extend our bot with the use of other **application program interfaces** (**APIs**). This means teaching our bot how to listen for keywords, respond to commands, and deal with errors (human or otherwise). In this chapter, we will cover the following:

- Responding to keywords
- Bot commands
- External API integration
- Error handling

Responding to keywords

In the previous chapter, we used regular expressions to test the contents of the message against some predefined keywords. Once the keywords were confirmed, we could perform actions and return the results. This worked well; however, it can lead to a large `if else` block for more feature-rich bots. Instead, we will now look at refactoring the end result of the previous chapter into a more modular design. In this section, we will accomplish this by using ES6's new `class` syntax and Node's `export` method.

Using classes

Start by creating a new JavaScript file and name it `bot.js`. Paste the following into `bot.js` and save the file:

```
'use strict';

const RtmClient = require('@slack/client').RtmClient;
const MemoryDataStore = require('@slack/client').MemoryDataStore;
```

```
const CLIENT_EVENTS = require('@slack/client').CLIENT_EVENTS;
const RTM_EVENTS = require('@slack/client').RTM_EVENTS;

class Bot {
  constructor(opts) {
    let slackToken = opts.token;
    let autoReconnect = opts.autoReconnect || true;
    let autoMark = opts.autoMark || true;

    this.slack = new RtmClient(slackToken, {
      // Sets the level of logging we require
      logLevel: 'error',
      // Initialize a data store for our client,
      // this will load additional helper
      // functions for the storing and retrieval of data
      dataStore: new MemoryDataStore(),
      // Boolean indicating whether Slack should automatically
      // reconnect after an error response
      autoReconnect: autoReconnect,
      // Boolean indicating whether each message should be marked
      // as read or not after it is processed
      autoMark: autoMark
    });

    this.slack.on(CLIENT_EVENTS.RTM.RTM_CONNECTION_OPENED, () => {
      let user =
      this.slack.dataStore.getUserById(this.slack.activeUserId)
      let team =
      this.slack.dataStore.getTeamById(this.slack.activeTeamId);

      this.name = user.name;

      console.log(`Connected to ${team.name} as ${user.name}`);
    });

    this.slack.start();
  }
}

// Export the Bot class, which will be imported when 'require' is
// used
module.exports = Bot;
```

Let's look at the code in depth, starting with the `class` structure. The **Mozilla Developer Network (MDN)** defines JavaScript classes as:

> *JavaScript classes are introduced in ECMAScript 6 and are syntactical sugar over JavaScript's existing prototype-based inheritance. The class syntax is not introducing a new object-oriented inheritance model to JavaScript. JavaScript classes provide a much simpler and clearer syntax to create objects and deal with inheritance.*

Simply put, JavaScript classes are an *alternative* to the prototype-based class pattern, and in fact function the exact same way under the hood. The benefit to using classes is when you wish to extend or inherit from a particular class, or provide a clearer overview of what your class does.

In the code example, we use a class in order to easily extend it later if we wish to add more functionality. Unique to classes is the `constructor` method, which is a special method for creating and initializing an object created with a class. When a class is called with the new keyword, this constructor function is what gets executed first:

```
constructor(opts) {
    let slackToken = opts.token;
    let autoReconnect = opts.autoReconnect || true;
    let autoMark = opts.autoMark || true;

    this.slack = new RtmClient(slackToken, {
      logLevel: 'error',
      dataStore: new MemoryDataStore(),
      autoReconnect: autoReconnect,
      autoMark: autoMark
    });

    this.slack.on(CLIENT_EVENTS.RTM.RTM_CONNECTION_OPENED, () => {
      let user = this.slack.dataStore.
      getUserById(this.slack.activeUserId)
      let team = this.slack.dataStore.
      getTeamById(this.slack.activeTeamId);

      this.name = user.name;

      console.log(`Connected to ${team.name} as ${user.name}`);
    });

    this.slack.start();
  }
```

Looking at our constructor, we see the familiar use of the Slack RTM client: the client is initialized and the `RTM_CONNECTION_OPENED` event is used to log the team and username upon connecting. We attach the `slack` variable to the `this` object as a property, making it accessible throughout our class. Similarly, we assign the bot's name to a variable, for easy access when required.

Finally, we export the bot class via the Node modules system:

```
module.exports = Bot;
```

This instructs Node to return our class when this file is imported using the `require` method.

Create a new file in the same folder as `bot.js` and name it `index.js`. Paste the following inside it:

```
'use strict';

let Bot = require('./Bot');

const bot = new Bot({
  token: process.env.SLACK_TOKEN,
  autoReconnect: true,
  autoMark: true
});
```

After saving the file, run the following from the terminal to start the bot:

SLACK_TOKEN=[YOUR_TOKEN_HERE] node index.js

You can use the Slack token created in the previous chapter, or generate a new one for this bot.

 It's generally a good idea to not hardcode sensitive information such as tokens or API keys (such as the Slack token) in your code. Instead, use Node's `process.env` object to pass variables from the command line to your code. Especially, take care of storing API keys in a public source control repository such as GitHub.

Once you've confirmed that your bot connects successfully to your Slack team, let's work on making the `Bot` class more modular.

Reactive bots

All the functionality described in our bot examples so far have one thing in common: the bots react to stimuli provided by human users. A message containing a keyword is sent and the bot responds with an action. These types of bot can be called reactive bots; they respond to an input with an output. The majority of bots can be classified as reactive bots, as most bots require some input in order to complete an action. An active bot is the opposite of this; rather than responding to input, the active bot produces output without needing any human stimuli. We will cover active bots in *Chapter 6*, *Webhooks and Slack Commands*. For now, let's look at how we can optimize our reactive bots.

We already defined the essential mechanism of reactive bots: responding to stimuli. As this is a core concept of the reactive bot, it makes sense to have a mechanism in place to easily invoke the desired behavior.

To do this, let's add some functionality to our `Bot` class in the form of a `respondsTo` function. In previous examples, we used the `if` statements to determine when a bot should respond to a message:

```
if (/(hello|hi) (bot|awesomebot)/g.test(msg)) {
  // do stuff...
}

if (/uptime/g.test(msg)) {
  // do more stuff...
}
```

There is nothing wrong with this approach. If we wish to code a bot that has multiple keywords, our `Bot` class can get very complex and cluttered very quickly. Instead, let's abstract out this behavior to our `respondsTo` function. The function should take at least two arguments: the keywords we wish to listen for and a callback function that executes when the keywords are identified in a message.

In `bot.js`, add the following to the constructor:

```
// Create an ES6 Map to store our regular expressions
this.keywords = new Map();

this.slack.on(RTM_EVENTS.MESSAGE, (message) => {
  // Only process text messages
  if (!message.text) {
    return;
  }
```

```
      let channel =
      this.slack.dataStore.getChannelGroupOrDMById(message.channel);
      let user = this.slack.dataStore.getUserById(message.user);

      // Loop over the keys of the keywords Map object and test each
      // regular expression against the message's text property
      for (let regex of this.keywords.keys()) {
        if (regex.test(message.text)) {
          let callback = this.keywords.get(regex);
          callback(message, channel, user);
        }
      }
    });
```

This snippet uses the new ES6 `Map` object, which is a simple key/value store, much like dictionaries in other languages. `Map` differs from `Object` in that `Map` does not have default keys (as `Object` has a prototype), which means that you can iterate over a `Map` without having to explicitly check if the `Map` contains a value or if its prototype does. For example, with `Maps`, you no longer have to use `Object.hasOwnProperty` when iterating.

As we will see later, the `keywords` `Map` object uses regular expressions as a key and a callback function as the value. Insert the following code underneath the constructor function:

```
respondTo(keywords, callback, start) {
    // If 'start' is truthy, prepend the '^' anchor to instruct the
    // expression to look for matches at the beginning of the string
    if (start) {
      keywords = '^' + keywords;
    }

    // Create a new regular expression, setting the case
    // insensitive (i) flag
    let regex = new RegExp(keywords, 'i');

    // Set the regular expression to be the key, with the callback
    // function as the value
    this.keywords.set(regex, callback);
}
```

This function takes three parameters: `keywords`, `callback`, and `start`. `keywords` is the word or phrase we wish to act on in the form of a regular expression. `callback` is a function that will be called if the keywords match the message, and `start` is an optional Boolean indicating whether we wish to search only at the beginning of the message string or not.

Look back at our newly updated constructor and pay special attention to the following lines within our `message` event listener:

```
// Loop over the keys of the keywords Map object and test each
// regular expression against the message's text property
for (let regex of this.keywords.keys()) {
  if (regex.test(message.text)) {
    let callback = this.keywords.get(regex);
    callback(message, channel, user);
  }
}
```

Here, we loop through the keywords `Map` object, which has regular expressions as its keys. We test each regular expression against the received message and call our callback function with the message, the channel, and the user that sent the message.

Finally, let's add a `sendMessage` functionality to our bot class. This will act as a wrapper for Slack's `sendMessage`. We don't have to expose the entire Slack object anymore. Add the following function underneath our constructor:

```
// Send a message to a channel, with an optional callback
send(message, channel, cb) {
  this.slack.sendMessage(message, channel.id, () => {
    if (cb) {
      cb();
    }
  });
}
```

Despite having `channel` as an argument name, our `send` function will also work for a DM (a private channel between two people), additionally providing a callback via the Slack API's `sendMessage` function.

Now that we have a function that can subscribe to messages and their contents, open up `index.js` and let's add a simple "Hello World" implementation:

```
'use strict';

let Bot = require('./Bot');

const bot = new Bot({
  token: process.env.SLACK_TOKEN,
  autoReconnect: true,
  autoMark: true
});
```

```
bot.respondTo('hello', (message, channel, user) => {
    bot.send(`Hello to you too, ${user.name}!`, channel)
}, true);
```

Save the file, restart your node process, and test out your bot. Here's what it should look like:

paul 17:56
hello

awesomebot BOT 17:56
Hello to you too, paul!

paul 17:56
a message with hello in it, but not at the beginning

Testing our refactor

The bot responds when our message has the string "hello", but only when it appears at the beginning of the message due to the `true` value we passed in after our callback.

We have now refactored our bot's code to abstract the Slack event system away and make our code cleaner in the process. Let's do something a little more impressive with our new system and implement a simple game.

Bot commands

So far, our bots have responded to keywords in messages to say hello or tell us how long they've been running. These keywords are useful for simple tasks, but for more complex actions, we need to give the bot some parameters to work with. A keyword followed by parameters or arguments can be referred to as a bot command. Similar to the command line, we can issue as many arguments as we want to get the most out of our bot.

Let's test this by giving our bot a new function: a game of chance where the issuer of the `roll` command plays a game of who can roll the highest number.

Add the following code to `index.js`:

```
bot.respondTo('roll', (message, channel, user) => {
  // get the arguments from the message body
  let args = getArgs(message.text);

  // Roll two random numbers between 0 and 100
  let firstRoll = Math.round(Math.random() * 100);
  let secondRoll = Math.round(Math.random() * 100);

  let challenger = user.name;
  let opponent = args[0];

  // reroll in the unlikely event that it's a tie
  while (firstRoll === secondRoll) {
    secondRoll = Math.round(Math.random() * 100);
  }

  let winner = firstRoll > secondRoll ? challenger : opponent;

  // Using new line characters (\n) to format our response
  bot.send(
    `${challenger} fancies their chances against ${opponent}!\n
    ${challenger} rolls: ${firstRoll}\n
    ${opponent} rolls: ${secondRoll}\n\n
    *${winner} is the winner!*`
  , channel);

}, true);

// Take the message text and return the arguments
function getArgs(msg) {
  return msg.split(' ').slice(1);
}
```

The command is very simple: a user sends the keyword `roll` followed by the name of the user they wish to challenge. This is shown in the following screenshot:

paul 22:05
roll awesomebot

awesomebot BOT 22:05
paul fancies their chances against awesomebot!

paul rolls: 53

awesomebot rolls: 11

paul is the winner!

A straightforward implementation of the bot's roll command

It works well, but what happens if we omit any arguments to our `roll` command?

paul 22:07
roll

awesomebot BOT 22:07
paul fancies their chances against undefined!

paul rolls: 4

undefined rolls: 77

undefined is the winner!

`undefined` wins the game, which isn't expected behavior

No arguments are provided; therefore, the value at index 0 of our `args` array is `undefined`. Clearly, our bot lacks some basic functionality: invalid argument error handling.

With bot commands, user input must always be sanitized and checked for errors, lest the bot perform some unwanted actions.

Sanitizing inputs

Add this block underneath our `getArgs` method call to stop empty rolls from happening:

```
// if args is empty, return with a warning
if (args.length < 1) {
  channel.send('You have to provide the name of the person you
  wish to challenge!');
  return;
}
```

Here's the result:

 paul 12:22
roll

 awesomebot BOT 12:22
You have to provide the name of the person you wish to challenge!

Awesomebot providing some necessary sanitizing

That's one use case down, but what if someone tries to challenge someone who's not in the channel? At the moment, the bot will roll against whatever you put as the first argument, be it a member of the channel or a complete fabrication. This is an example of where we want to further sanitize and restrict the user input to useful data.

To fix this, let's make sure that only members of the channel from where the `roll` command originated can be targeted.

First, let's add the following method to our `Bot` class:

```
getMembersByChannel(channel) {
    // If the channel has no members then that means we're in a DM
    if (!channel.members) {
      return false;
    }
```

```
    // Only select members which are active and not a bot
    let members = channel.members.filter((member) => {
      let m = this.slack.dataStore.getUserById(member);
      // Make sure the member is active (i.e. not set to 'away'
      status)
      return (m.presence === 'active' && !m.is_bot);
    });

    // Get the names of the members
    members = members.map((member) => {
      return this.slack.dataStore.getUserById(member).name;
    });

    return members;
  }
```

This function simply checks to see whether the members property of channel exists, and returns a list of active non-bot users by name. In index.js, replace your roll command block with the following code:

```
bot.respondTo('roll', (message, channel, user) => {
  // get the members of the channel
  const members = bot.getMembersByChannel(channel);

  // make sure there actually members to interact with. If there
  // aren't then it usually means that the command was given in a
  // direct message
  if (!members) {
    bot.send('You have to challenge someone in a channel, not a
    direct message!', channel);
    return;
  }

  // get the arguments from the message body
  let args = getArgs(message.text);

  // if args is empty, return with a warning
  if (args.length < 1) {
    bot.send('You have to provide the name of the person you wish
    to challenge!', channel);
    return;
  }
```

```
// does the opponent exist in this channel?
if (members.indexOf(args[0]) < 0) {
  bot.send(`Sorry ${user.name}, but I either can't find
  ${args[0]} in this channel, or they are a bot!`, channel);
  return;
}

// Roll two random numbers between 0 and 100
let firstRoll = Math.round(Math.random() * 100);
let secondRoll = Math.round(Math.random() * 100);

let challenger = user.name;
let opponent = args[0];

// reroll in the unlikely event that it's a tie
while (firstRoll === secondRoll) {
  secondRoll = Math.round(Math.random() * 100);
}

let winner = firstRoll > secondRoll ? challenger : opponent;

// Using new line characters (\n) to format our response
bot.send(
  `${challenger} fancies their changes against ${opponent}!\n
  ${challenger} rolls: ${firstRoll}\n
  ${opponent} rolls: ${secondRoll}\n\n
  *${winner} is the winner!*`
, channel);

}, true);
```

Our biggest changes here are that the bot will now check to make sure the command given is a valid one. It will ensure that by checking the following (listed in order):

1. There are members available in the channel.

2. An argument was provided after the command.

3. Whether the argument was valid, by making sure the name provided is in the members list of the channel or that the name is not that of a bot.

The important lesson to take away from this exercise is to minimize interruptions by ensuring that all use cases are handled correctly. Sufficient testing is required to be certain that you handled all use cases. For instance, in our `roll` command example, we missed an important case: users can use the `roll` command against themselves:

Rolling against yourself probably isn't the most useful of functions

To fix this issue, we need to make a simple addition to our command. Add the following code in our previous sanitizing checks:

```
// the user shouldn't challenge themselves
if (args.indexOf(user.name) > -1) {
  bot.send(`Challenging yourself is probably not the best use of
  your or my time, ${user.name}`, channel);
  return;
}
```

When developing bots, every precaution should be taken to ensure that bot inputs are sanitized and that error responses give information about the error. This is especially true when working with external APIs, where incorrect input could lead to wildly inaccurate results.

External API integration

Eternal APIs are third-party services hosted outside of our bot structure. These come in many varying types and are used to solve many different problems, but their use in tandem with bots follows the same data flow structure.

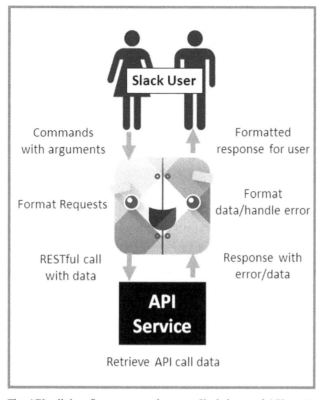

The API call data flow structure between Slack, bot, and API service

We will build an example bot with API integration using a common and free-to-use API, namely that of the Wikimedia foundation.

 Be warned that while many APIs are free, there are many that charge when a certain amount of requests are made. Always check whether there is a fee before incorporating them into your bots.

The Wikimedia foundation API is an example of a **representational state transfer (REST)** service, which communicates using standard **Hypertext Transfer Protocol (HTTP)** protocols such as GET or POST. Many RESTful services require you to transmit a token along with your request, ensuring security and for monetizing the service by tracking the amount of requests made. The Wikimedia API is a free RESTful service, meaning that we do not require a token to make use of it.

Our new bot, wikibot, will allow the user to search for a Wikipedia page and return the page's summary if found, or an error message if it does not exist.

To start, you should follow the steps in *Chapter 2, Your First Bot*, to create a new Slack bot integration via the Slack web service and start a new project. This new project will reuse the `Bot` class created in this chapter, whereas our new `index.js` entry point will be a new, empty file.

We will start with the annotated and explained `index.js` code. At the conclusion of the chapter the full code will be made available for easier accessibility. Here's the code:

```
'use strict';

const Bot = require('./Bot');
const request = require('superagent');
```

Here, we import our own `Bot` class alongside a new library called `superagent`, which is used for making asynchronous JavaScript and XML (AJAX) calls.

Before running this code, be sure to install `superagent` using NPM:

npm install superagent --save

`superagent` is installed with the `-save` flag, as the program cannot function without it.

Let's get back to our code:

```
const wikiAPI =
"https://en.wikipedia.org/w/api.php?format=json&action=query&prop=
extracts&exintro=&explaintext=&titles="
const wikiURL = 'https://en.wikipedia.org/wiki/';
```

These constants are the RESTful API **Uniform Resource Link (URL)** and the base Wikipedia page URL, respectively. You can test out the former by copying the URL, pasting it into the address field in a browser, and appending a topic at the end. You can check this for the following URL: `https://en.wikipedia.org/w/api.php?for mat=json&action=query&prop=extracts&exintro=&explaintext=&titles=duck`.

You should then see data returned in the **JavaScript object notation (JSON)** format, giving you an overview of the topic requested and the pages returned. The data and type of data returned is determined by the parameters in the query string of the URL. In the preceding URL, we query for the `extracts` property of a page, specifically the intro (`exintro`) and explanation (`explaintext`) for the page with the title `duck` in the JSON format.

The latter constant is used later to return the URL for the Wikipedia page requested:

```
const bot = new Bot({
  token: process.env.SLACK_TOKEN,
  autoReconnect: true,
  autoMark: true
});
```

As before, we initiate a new instance of `Bot` with our options and Slack token. You can reuse the first token created in *Chapter 2, Your First Bot*. However, it is recommended to generate a new one instead. The code is as follows:

```
function getWikiSummary(term, cb) {
  // replace spaces with unicode
  let parameters = term.replace(/ /g, '%20');
```

This function is a wrapper for the request to the Wikimedia API, in which we format the request by replacing the spaces in the search term with Unicode and make the GET request via the `superagent` library. The code is as follows:

```
request
  .get(wikiAPI + parameters)
  .end((err, res) => {
    if (err) {
      cb(err);
      return;
    }

    let url = wikiURL + parameters;

    cb(null, JSON.parse(res.text), url);
  });
}
```

As this is an asynchronous request, we provide a callback function to be called when the GET request has returned the data we need. Before returning we make sure to parse the data into a JavaScript object form for easy access. The code is as follows:

```
bot.respondTo('help', (message, channel) => {
  bot.send(`To use my Wikipedia functionality, type \`wiki\`
  followed by your search query`, channel);
}, true);
```

paul 17:28
help

wikibot BOT 17:28
To use my Wikipedia functionality, type `wiki` followed by your search query

Wikibot explaining how it can be used

The first command we implement is a simple `help` command; its only function is to explain how to use the bot's Wikipedia functionality:

```
bot.respondTo('wiki', (message, channel, user) => {
  if (user && user.is_bot) {
    return;
  }
}
```

Set up our new bot command with the keyword `wiki` and make sure to return if the command sender is a bot:

```
// grab the search parameters, but remove the command 'wiki'
// from
// the beginning of the message first
let args = message.text.split(' ').slice(1).join(' ');
```

This will extract the search query of the command. For instance if the command is `wiki fizz buzz`, the output of `args` will be a string containing "fizz buzz":

```
getWikiSummary(args, (err, result, url) => {
  if (err) {
    bot.send(`I\'m sorry, but something went wrong with your
    query`, channel);
    console.error(err);
    return;
  }
}
```

Here, we call our `getWikiSummary` function, with the arguments issued with the bot command and provide the anonymous function callback. If an error has occurred, immediately send an error message and log the error in the console. The command is as follows:

```
let pageID = Object.keys(result.query.pages)[0];
```

The data object returned by the RESTful API call consists of a nested object named `query`, which in turn has a nested object called `pages`. Inside the `pages` object, there are more objects that use Wikipedia's internal page ID as a key, which is a series of numbers in a string format. Let's take a look at an example:

```json
{
  "batchcomplete": "",
  "query": {
    "normalized": [
      {
        "from": "duck",
        "to": "Duck"
      }
    ],
    "pages": {
      "37674": {
        "pageid": 37674,
        "ns": 0,
        "title": "Duck",
        "extract": "Duck is the common name for a large number of species in the waterfowl family Anatidae, which also includes swans and geese. The ducks are divided among several subfamilies in the family Anatidae; they do not represent a monophyletic group (the group of all descendants of a single common ancestral species) but a form taxon, since swans and geese are not considered ducks. Ducks are mostly aquatic birds, mostly smaller than the swans and geese, and may be found in both fresh water and sea water.\nDucks are sometimes confused with several types of unrelated water birds with similar forms, such as loons or divers, grebes, gallinules, and coots.\n\n"
      }
    }
  }
}
```

`Object.keys` is a useful trick to retrieve data from an object without knowing the property's name. We use it here as we don't know the key ID for the page that we want, but we know we want the first value. `Object.keys` will return an array of key names for the `result.query.pages` object. We then select the value at index 0, as we're only interested in the first result. The code is as follows:

```
// -1 indicates that the article doesn't exist
if (parseInt(pageID, 10) === -1) {
    bot.send('That page does not exist yet, perhaps you\'d like
    to create it:', channel);
    bot.send(url, channel);
    return;
}
```

A Wikipedia page ID of -1 indicates that the article doesn't exist at all. Instead of trying to parse data that doesn't exist, we inform the user of the problem and return. The code is as follows:

```
let page = result.query.pages[pageID];
let summary = page.extract;

if (/may refer to/i.test(summary)) {
    bot.send('Your search query may refer to multiple things,
    please be more specific or visit:', channel);
    bot.send(url, channel);
    return;
}
```

If the summary text contains the phrase `may refer to`, then we can conclude that the search term provided could lead to multiple Wikipedia entries. Since we can't guess at what the user intended, we simply ask them to be more specific and return. The code is as follows:

```
if (summary !== '') {
    bot.send(url, channel);
```

Unfortunately, it is possible that an API request returns a summary that is empty. This is an issue on the Wikimedia API's end where a term returns a page, but the summary text is missing. In this case, we inform the user of the problem in the `else` conditional block of this `if` statement. The code is as follows:

```
let paragraphs = summary.split('\n');
```

The summary might stretch over several paragraphs, so for ease of use we convert the text block into an array of paragraphs by using the new line ASCII operator \n as our split criteria. The code is as follows:

```
paragraphs.forEach((paragraph) => {
  if (paragraph !== '') {
    bot.send(`> ${paragraph}`, channel);
  }
});
```

Like regular users, bots can use Slack's formatting options when sending messages. In this instance, we prepend the > operator in front of our paragraph to indicate a quotation block. The code is as follows:

```
} else {
      bot.send('I\'m sorry, I couldn\'t find anything on that
        subject. Try another one!', channel);
    }
  });
}, true);
```

As before, we pass the true Boolean to our respondsTo method of the Bot class to indicate that we want our keyword wiki to only trigger a response if it is placed at the beginning of a message.

Once you've entered all the code into index.js, run the program using Node and test it in your Slack client:

Wikibot is up and running

This is a basic example of how to incorporate external API calls into your bot. Before we move on to the next section, we should consider the ramifications of complex API requests. If an API request takes a sizeable amount of time (for example, a service needs to perform complex calculations), it would be useful for the user to see an indication that the bot is working on the command. To accomplish this, we can show a **typing indicator** while the bot waits for a response. Typing indicators are shown when a human starts to type a message before hitting send. Add the following method to the `Bot` class in `bot.js`:

```
setTypingIndicator(channel) {
    this.slack.send({ type: 'typing', channel: channel.id });
}
```

To test our indicator, add the following to `index.js`:

```
bot.respondTo('test', (message, channel) => {
    bot.setTypingIndicator(message.channel);

    setTimeout(() => {
        bot.send('Not typing anymore!', channel);
    }, 1000);
}, true);
```

Now, send the message `test` in your Slack channel and watch the indicator appear:

Wikibot is busy typing

1000 milliseconds later, we get the following result:

Bot is done with the action and the typing indicator has been removed

After the typing indicator is dispatched, it will automatically disappear once a message has been sent to the channel by the bot.

To use the typing indicator in our example bot, insert the following line above the getWikiSummary method call:

```
bot.setTypingIndicator(message.channel);
```

Keep in mind that since the Wikimedia API call resolves very quickly, it's unlikely that you'll see the typing indicator for longer than a few milliseconds.

Error handling

Continuing on from the last topic, a good way of making your bot appear more natural is for it to provide clear instructions on how to use it. Providing the wrong input for a command should *never* cause the bot to crash.

 Bots should never crash due to user input. Either an error message should be sent or the request should silently fail.

You can eliminate 99 percent of all bugs in your bot commands by doing valid type and content checking against the user's input. Observe the following checklist when programming a new command:

- If arguments are required, are any of the arguments undefined?
- Are the arguments of the type the bot is expecting? For example, are strings provided when a number is expected?

- If targeting a member of the channel, does that member exist?

- Was the command sent in a DM? If so should the command still be executed?

- Does the command pass a "sanity" check? For example, does the data or action requested make sense?

As an example of the preceding checklist, let's review the checks we made with the `roll` command earlier in this chapter:

- Are there non-bot members in the channel to interact with?

- Was an argument supplied?

- Was the supplied argument valid?

- Is the specified opponent in the channel the command was issued?

Each point is a hurdle that the command's input had to overcome in order to return the desired result. If any of these questions is answered in the negative, then an error message is sent and the command process terminated.

These checks might appear lengthy and superfluous, but they are absolutely necessary to provide a natural experience with the bot.

As a final note, be aware that despite your best efforts, users have an uncanny ability to cause crashes, intentionally or otherwise.

The more complex your bot becomes, the more likely it is that loopholes and edge cases will appear. Testing your bot thoroughly will get you most of the way, but always make sure that you are catching and logging errors on the programmatic side. A good debug log will save you many hours of frustration trying to find a difficult-to-squash bug.

Summary

In this chapter, we saw how to abstract away the core Slack API methods into a reusable module by using ES6's new class structures. The difference between a reactive and active bot was outlined as well as the distinction between keywords and bot commands. By applying the basic knowledge of external APIs outlined in this chapter, you should be able to create a bot that interfaces with any third-party application that provides RESTful APIs.

In the next chapter, we will learn about the Redis data storage service and how to write a bot that interfaces with a persistent data source.

4
Using Data

Now that we've seen how to process keywords, commands, and API calls, we will look at the next logical step in bot building: persistent data storage and retrieval. References to data can be kept in JavaScript by assigning said data to a variable; however, its use is limited to when the program is running. If the program is stopped or restarted, we lose the data. Hence, persistent data storage is required for certain tasks.

This allows us to build bots that can, for instance, keep track of a leaderboard or store a to-do list.

In this chapter, we will cover:

- Introduction to Redis
- Connecting to Redis
- Saving and retrieving data
- Best practices
- Error handling

Introduction to Redis

In the previous chapter, we discovered how to create a competitive roll bot that allows users to play a "Who can roll the highest" game. Although it worked admirably, the feature sorely missing is a leaderboard of sorts, where each user's wins and losses are stored and an overall winners list is kept.

Such a feature wouldn't be difficult to produce; however, the largest problem comes in storing the data. Any data stored in JavaScript variables would be lost once the program ends or crashes. A better solution would then be to maintain a persistent database, which our bot can write to and read from.

There is a wide variety of database services to choose from; you might already be familiar with MySQL or MongoDB. For the example bots in this chapter, we will pick a service that is easy to set up and simple to use.

The database service we will use is Redis: http://redis.io/.

The Redis website describes the technology as follows:

> *"Redis is an open source (BSD licensed), in-memory data structure store, used as database, cache and message broker. It supports data structures such as strings, hashes, lists, sets, sorted sets with range queries, bitmaps, hyperloglogs and geospatial indexes with radius queries. Redis has built-in replication, Lua scripting, LRU eviction, transactions, and different levels of on-disk persistence, and provides high availability via Redis Sentinel and automatic partitioning with Redis Cluster."*

A simpler explanation is that Redis is an efficient in-memory key-value store. Keys can be simple strings, hashes, lists (an ordered collection), sets (unordered collection of non-repeating values), or sorted sets (ordered or ranked collection of non-repeating values). Despite the complex official description, setting up and using Redis is a quick and painless process.

Redis' advantages are its impressive speed, cross-platform communication, and simplicity.

 Getting started with Redis is simple, but we will only be exploring the tip of the Redis iceberg. For more information on advanced uses of Redis, visit the Redis website.

There are many Redis client implementations written in a wide variety of languages (http://redis.io/clients), but we will use a Node-based Redis client.

Bear in mind that Redis is but one solution to the persistent data problem. Other solutions might include the use of a MySQL relational or a MongoDB non-relational database.

Installing Redis

To connect to Redis, we will use the Node Redis package. First, we must install and run our Redis server so Node will have something to connect to. Follow the instructions for your operating system of choice.

Mac OS X

The simplest way to install Redis is through the `homebrew` package manager. `homebrew` makes it easy to install applications and services through the command line.

If you are unable to use `homebrew`, visit the Redis quick start guide to install Redis manually: (`http://redis.io/topics/quickstart`).

If you are unsure whether you have Homebrew installed, open a terminal and run the following:

```
which brew
```

If nothing returns, run the following in your terminal:

```
/usr/bin/ruby -e "$(curl -fsSL https://raw.githubusercontent.com/
Homebrew/install/master/install)"
```

Follow the onscreen prompts until `homebrew` is successfully installed. To install Redis, run the following:

```
brew install redis
```

Once the installation has completed, you can start a Redis server by using the following command in your terminal:

```
redis-server
```

Windows

Visit the official Microsoft GitHub project for Redis and grab the latest release here: `https://github.com/MSOpenTech/redis/releases`. Once unzipped, you can run `redis-server.exe` to start the service and `redis-cli.exe` to connect to the server through the shell.

Unix

Refer to the Redis quickstart page for instructions on how to install on Linux/Unix systems: `http://redis.io/topics/quickstart`.

Once installed, you can start the server with the `redis-server` command and connect to the server via `redis-cli`. These commands function in the exact same way on OS X.

Now that Redis is installed, start the service and you should see something like this:

```
15907:C 09 Feb 22:28:54.963 # Warning: no config file specified, using the default config. In order to specify a confi
g file use redis-server /path/to/redis.conf
15907:M 09 Feb 22:28:54.965 * Increased maximum number of open files to 10032 (it was originally set to 256).


                                        Redis 3.0.6 (00000000/0) 64 bit

                                        Running in standalone mode
                                        Port: 6379
                                        PID: 15907


                                        http://redis.io






15907:M 09 Feb 22:28:54.967 # Server started, Redis version 3.0.6
15907:M 09 Feb 22:28:54.967 * DB loaded from disk: 0.000 seconds
15907:M 09 Feb 22:28:54.967 * The server is now ready to accept connections on port 6379
```

Redis successfully starting a server

Redis is now up and ready to be used on the default port 6379. Other ports may be used instead, but the default port is sufficient for our purposes.

Connecting to Redis

To demonstrate how to connect to Redis, we will create a new bot project (including the Bot class defined in *Chapter 3, Adding Complexity*). We'll start by installing the Redis Node client, executing the following:

npm install redis

Now, create a new index.js file and paste in the following code:

```
'use strict';

const redis = require('redis');
const Bot = require('./Bot');

const client = redis.createClient();

const bot = new Bot({
  token: process.env.SLACK_TOKEN,
  autoReconnect: true,
```

```
    autoMark: true
});

client.on('error', (err) => {
    console.log('Error ' + err);
});

client.on('connect', () => {
  console.log('Connected to Redis!');
});
```

This snippet will import the Redis client and connect to the local instance running via the `createClient()` method. When not supplied with any arguments, the aforementioned method will assume the service is running locally on the default port of 6379. If you wish to connect to a different host and port combination, then you can supply them with following:

```
let client = redis.createClient(port, host);
```

 For the purposes of this book, we will be using an unsecure Redis server. Without authentication or other security measures, your data could be accessed and edited by anyone who connects to your data service. If you intend to use Redis in a production environment, it is strongly recommended you read up on Redis security.

Next, ensure that you have the Redis client running in a different terminal window and start up our bot in the usual way:

SLACK_TOKEN=[your_token_here] node index.js

If all goes well, you should be greeted by this happy message:

```
[Thu Feb 11 2016 19:23:32 GMT-0500 (EST)] INFO Connecting...
Connected to Redis!
Connected to Building Bots as awesomebot
```

Our Node app has successfully connected to the local Redis server

As promised, setting up and connecting to Redis was an easy and quick endeavor. Next, we will look at actually setting and getting data from our server.

Saving and retrieving data

First, let's look at what the Redis client has to offer us. Add the following lines to index.js:

```
client.set('hello', 'Hello World!');

client.get('hello', (err, reply) => {
  if (err) {
    console.log(err);
    return;
  }

  console.log(`Retrieved: ${reply}`);
});
```

In this example, we will set the value "Hello world!" in Redis with the key hello. In the get command, we specify the key we wish to use to retrieve a value.

 The Node Redis client is entirely **asynchronous**. This means that you have to supply a callback function with each command if you wish to process data.

A common mistake is to use the Node Redis client in a synchronous way. Here's an example:

```
let val = client.get('hello');
console.log('val:', val);
```

This, perhaps confusingly, results in:

val: false

This is because the get function will have returned the Boolean false before the request to the Redis server has been made.

Run the correct code and you should see the successful retrieval of the **Hello world!** data:

```
Connected to Redis!
Retrieved: Hello World!
```

Our stored value is successfully retrieved

The maximum file size of a Redis string is 512 megabytes. If you need to store something larger than this, consider using multiple key/value pairings.

When developing Redis functionality, a good tip is to use the Redis client's built-in `print` command for easy debugging and testing:

```
client.set('hello', 'Hello World!', redis.print);

client.get('hello', redis.print);
```

This will print the following in the terminal:

Reply: OK

Reply: Hello World!

As we progress through the chapter, we will introduce more useful functions and methods provided by the Redis client. For a complete list and documentation, visit `https://github.com/NodeRedis/node_redis`.

Connecting bots

With our Redis server set up and the basic commands covered, let's apply what we've learned to a simple bot. In this example, we will code a bot that instructs the bot to *remember* a phrase based on a given key value.

Add the following code to your `index.js` file:

```
bot.respondTo('store', (message, channel, user) => {
  let msg = getArgs(message.text);

  client.set(user.name, msg, (err) => {
    if (err) {
      channel.send('Oops! I tried to store that but something went
      wrong :(');
    } else {
      channel.send(`Okay ${user.name}, I will remember that for
      you.`);
    }
  });
}, true);

bot.respondTo('retrieve', (message, channel, user) => {
  bot.setTypingIndicator(message.channel);
```

```
client.get(user.name, (err, reply) => {
  if (err) {
    console.log(err);
    return;
  }

  channel.send('Here\'s what I remember: ' + reply);
  });
});
```

Using the familiar `respondTo` command introduced in the `Bot` class of the previous chapter, we set up our bot to listen for the keyword `store` and then set that value in the Redis data store, using the message sender's name as a key. Let's see this in action:

Our bot remembers what we told it to

Notice how we use the callback function of the set method to ensure that the data was saved correctly, and informing the user if it was not.

While not terribly impressive behavior, the important thing to realize is that our bot has successfully stored values in the Redis data store. Redis will store the key value pairing on the local disk, which means that even if the bot and/or Redis server are stopped and started again the data will persist.

Dynamic storage

Once again, let's increase the complexity a bit. In the previous example, the key used to store data is always the command giver's name. In reality, this is impractical as it means a user could only store one thing at a time, overwriting the value each time they issued the command. In this next section, we will be augmenting our bot to allow the user to specify the key of the value to be stored, allowing for the storage of multiple values.

Delete the previous `respondsTo` commands and paste in the following snippets, noting the highlighted code:

```
bot.respondTo('store', (message, channel, user) => {
  let args = getArgs(message.text);

  let key = args.shift();
  let value = args.join(' ');

  client.set(key, value, (err) => {
    if (err) {
      channel.send('Oops! I tried to store something but
      something went wrong :(');
    } else {
      channel.send(`Okay ${user.name}, I will remember that for
      you.`);
    }
  });
}, true);

bot.respondTo('retrieve', (message, channel, user) => {
  bot.setTypingIndicator(message.channel);

  let key = getArgs(message.text).shift();

  client.get(key, (err, reply) => {
    if (err) {
      console.log(err);
      channel.send('Oops! I tried to retrieve something but
      something went wrong :(');
      return;
    }

    channel.send('Here\'s what I remember: ' + reply);
  });
});
```

In this interpretation, we expect the user to provide a command in the following format:

`store [key] [value]`

To extract the key and value from the command, we first use JavaScript's `Array.shift` to remove and return the value at index 0 of the `args` array. Then, it's a simple case of collecting the rest of the arguments as the value by using `Array.join`. Now, we apply what we learned in the previous section to store the user-defined key and value in the Redis instance.

When the `retrieve` command is given, we use the same `Array.shift` technique to extract the key requested. We will then use it to retrieve the stored data. Let's see it is in action:

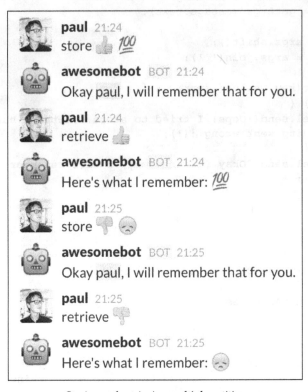

Storing and retrieving multiple entities

 Emojis within a message's text are converted into their basic text components. For instance, the thumbs up emoji is translated to `:+1`. This conversion works both ways, which means that Slack will automatically render any emoji text the bot sends.

Hashes, lists, and sets

So far, we've used a single data type for our keys and values: strings. While keys are limited to string values, Redis allows for the value to be a variety of different data types. The different types are as follows:

- String
- Hash

- List
- Set
- Sorted set

We are already familiar with strings, so let's work down the list and explain the different data types.

Hashes

Hashes are similar to JavaScript objects. However, they differ in that Redis hashes do not support nested objects. All the property values of a hash will be cast to strings. Take the following JavaScript object:

```
let obj = {
  foo: 'bar',
  baz: {
    foobar: 'bazfoo'
  }
};
```

The `baz` property contains an object, and we can store the `obj` object in Redis by using the `hmset` function:

```
client.hmset('obj', obj);
```

Then, we retrieve the data with `hgetall`:

```
client.hgetall('obj', (err, object) => {
  console.log(object);
});
```

This will log the following line in our terminal:

```
{ foo: 'bar', baz: '[object Object]' }
```

Redis has stored the nested `baz` object by first calling the `Object.toString()` function on it, which means that the string value is returned when we perform our `hgetall` function.

A workaround is to leverage JavaScript's JSON object to stringify our nested object before storing and then parsing the object returned from Redis. Observe the following example:

```
let obj = {
  foo: 'bar',
  baz: {
    foobar: 'bazfoo'
```

```
    }
  };

  function stringifyNestedObjects(obj) {
    for (let k in obj) {
      if (obj[k] instanceof Object) {
        obj[k] = JSON.stringify(obj[k]);
      }
    }

    return obj;
  }

  function parseNestedObjects(obj) {
    for (let k in obj) {
      if (typeof obj[k] === 'string' || obj[k] instanceof String) {
        try {
          obj[k] = JSON.parse(obj[k]);
        } catch(e) {
          // string wasn't a stringified object, so fail silently
        }
      }
    }

    return obj;
  }

  client.hmset('obj', stringifyNestedObjects(obj));

  client.hgetall('obj', (err, object) => {
    console.log(parseNestedObjects(object));
  });
```

When executed, we see the logged result:

```
  { foo: 'bar', baz: { foobar: 'bazfoo' } }
```

> The examples given here only stringify and parse objects nested one level deep. In order to stringify and parse an object of *N* depth, look into the recursion programming technique. A good example can be found at https://msdn.microsoft.com/en-us/library/wwbyhkx4(v=vs.94).aspx.

Lists

Redis lists are functionally the same as JavaScript arrays. Like with objects, the value of every index is converted into a string when storing. When dealing with a multidimensional array (for example, an array containing a subset of arrays) the toString function will be called before storing in Redis. A simple Array.join(',') can be used to convert this string value back to an array.

The lpush and rpush commands can be used to store our list:

```
client.rpush('heroes', ['batman', 'superman', 'spider-man']);
```

In the preceding snippet, we are pushing our array of heroes to the right of the list. This works exactly the same as JavaScript's Array.push, where the new values are appended to the existing array. In this case, it means that previously empty list now contains our heroes array.

We can push to the left of the array to prepend to the list:

```
client.lpush('heroes', 'iron-man');
```

This will result in our list looking like so:

```
[ 'iron-man', 'batman', 'superman', 'spider-man' ]
```

Finally, to access our Redis list we can use the lrange method:

```
client.lrange('heroes', 0, -1, (err, list) => {
  console.log(list);
});
```

The second and third arguments provided to lrange are the selection start and end position. To return all the elements in the list rather than a subset, we can provide -1 as an end position.

Sets

Sets are similar to Redis lists with one very useful difference: sets do not allow duplicates. Consider the following example:

```
client.sadd('fruits', ['apples', 'bananas', 'oranges']);
client.sadd('fruits', 'bananas');

client.smembers('fruits', (err, set) => {
  console.log(set);
});
```

Here, we use the Redis client's `sadd` to store the set and `smembers` to retrieve it. In the second line, we attempt to add the fruit `'bananas'` to the `'fruits'` list, but since the value already exists, the `sadd` call silently fails. The retrieved set is as expected:

```
[ 'oranges', 'apples', 'bananas' ]
```

 You might notice that the ordering of the retrieved 'fruits' set is different from the order that it was stored in. This is because a set is built using `HashTable`, which means there are no guarantees to the order of the elements. If you want to store your elements in a particular order, you must use a list or a sorted set.

Sorted sets

Functioning as a sort of hybrid between lists and sets, sorted sets have a specific order and cannot contain duplicates. See the following example:

```
client.zadd('scores', [3, 'paul', 2, 'caitlin', 1, 'alex']);

client.zrange('scores', 0, -1, (err, set) => {
  console.log(set);
});

client.zrevrange('scores', 0, -1, 'withscores', (err, set) => {
  console.log(set);
});
```

Using the `zadd` method, we specify the key for our sorted set and an array of values. The array indicates the order of the stored set by following this format:

```
[ score, value, score, value ... ]
```

The `zrange` method uses similar arguments to `lrange`, we specify the start and end positions of the set to be returned. This method will return the set in ascending order:

```
[ 'alex', 'caitlin', 'paul' ]
```

We can reverse this by using `zrevrange`. Note how we also provide the `withscores` string as an argument. This argument will return the scores of each element:

```
[ 'paul', '3', 'caitlin', '2', 'alex', '1' ]
```

The withscores argument can be used for all sorted set retrieval methods.

As you might have realized already, sorted sets especially shine when used to keep track of game scores or leaderboards. With that in mind, let's revisit our "roll" bot from *Chapter 3, Adding Complexity*, and add a leaderboard of winners.

Best practices

Any user should be able to store data in Redis via bot commands; it is however recommended you ensure that the data storage methods cannot be easily abused. Accidental abuse might happen in the form of many different Redis calls in a short amount of time. For more information on Slack channel spam and remedies, revisit *Chapter 2, Your First Bot*.

By restricting bot traffic, we can ensure that Redis does not receive an inordinate amount of write and retrieve actions. If you ever find that Redis latency is not as good as it should be, visit this webpage to help troubleshoot: http://redis.io/topics/latency.

Let's now look at how we can improve familiar bot behavior with the addition of Redis data storage.

First, here is our roll command, with the new Redis store code highlighted:

```
bot.respondTo('roll', (message, channel, user) => {
  // get the members of the channel
  const members = bot.getMembersByChannel(channel);

  // make sure there actually members to interact with. If there
  // aren't then it usually means that the command was given in a
  // direct message
  if (!members) {
    channel.send('You have to challenge someone in a channel, not
    a direct message!');
    return;
  }

  // get the arguments from the message body
  let args = getArgs(message.text);
```

```
  // if args is empty, return with a warning
  if (args.length < 1) {
    channel.send('You have to provide the name of the person you
    wish to challenge!');
    return;
  }

  // the user shouldn't challenge themselves
  if (args.indexOf(user.name) > -1) {
    channel.send(`Challenging yourself is probably not the best
    use of your or my time, ${user.name}`);
    return;
  }

  // does the opponent exist in this channel?
  if (members.indexOf(args[0]) < 0) {
    channel.send(`Sorry ${user.name}, but I either can't find
    ${args[0]} in this channel, or they are a bot!`);
    return;
  }

  // Roll two random numbers between 0 and 100
  let firstRoll = Math.round(Math.random() * 100);
  let secondRoll = Math.round(Math.random() * 100);

  let challenger = user.name;
  let opponent = args[0];

  // reroll in the unlikely event that it's a tie
  while (firstRoll === secondRoll) {
    secondRoll = Math.round(Math.random() * 100);
  }

  let winner = firstRoll > secondRoll ? challenger : opponent;

  client.zincrby('rollscores', 1, winner);

  // Using new line characters (\n) to format our response
  channel.send(
    `${challenger} fancies their changes against ${opponent}!\n
    ${challenger} rolls: ${firstRoll}\n
    ${opponent} rolls: ${secondRoll}\n\n
    *${winner} is the winner!*`
  );

}, true);
```

To store the user's win, we use the Redis client's `zincrby` method, which will increment the winner's score by one. Note how we can specify how much to increment by in the second argument. If the key (the winner's name here) doesn't exist in the set, it is automatically created with the score 0 and then incremented by the specified amount.

To retrieve the scoreboard, lets add the following:

```
bot.respondTo('scoreboard', (message, channel) => {
  client.zrevrange('rollscores', 0, -1, 'withscores', (err, set)
  => {
    if (err) {
      channel.send('Oops, something went wrong! Please try again
      later');
      return;
    }

    let scores = [];

    // format the set into something a bit easier to use
    for (let i = 0; i < set.length; i++) {
      scores.push([set[i], set[i + 1]]);
      i++;
    }

    channel.send('The current scoreboard is:');
    scores.forEach((score, index) => {
      channel.send(`${index + 1}. ${score[0]} with ${score[1]}
      points.`);
    });
  });
}, true);
```

Once the `scoreboard` command is given, we immediately look for the reverse range by using the `zrevrange` method. This will asynchronously return an array in the format:

```
[ NAME, SCORE, NAME2, SCORE2, NAME3, SCORE3, …]
```

Next, we transform that array into a two-dimensional array by splitting the names and scores into nested arrays, which looks like this:

```
[ [NAME, SCORE], [NAME2, SCORE2], [NAME3, SCORE3], …]
```

Formatting the data in this way makes it easy for us to send the name and score to the channel, preceded by the placing on the scoreboard (the index of the array plus one).

The final result in Slack shows us a working scoreboard:

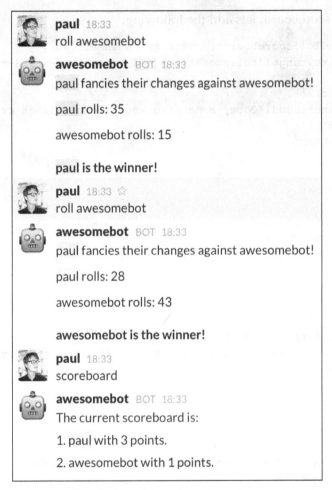

A scoreboard achieved through persistent data storage

Before moving on to another example, let's look at how to delete a Redis key/value pairing. Replace your `scoreboard` command with the following, taking note of the highlighted code:

```
bot.respondTo('scoreboard', (message, channel, user) => {
    let args = getArgs(message.text);

    if (args[0] === 'wipe') {
```

```
      client.del('rollscores');
      channel.send('The scoreboard has been wiped!');
      return;
   }

   client.zrevrange('rollscores', 0, -1, 'withscores', (err, set)
   => {
     if (err) {
       channel.send('Oops, something went wrong! Please try again
       later');
       return;
     }

     if (set.length < 1) {
       channel.send('No scores yet! Challenge each other with the
       \`roll\` command!');
       return;
     }

     let scores = [];

     // format the set into something a bit easier to use
     for (let i = 0; i < set.length; i++) {
       scores.push([set[i], set[i + 1]]);
       i++;
     }

     channel.send('The current scoreboard is:');
     scores.forEach((score, index) => {
       channel.send(`${index + 1}. ${score[0]} with ${score[1]}
       points.`);
     });
   });
 }, true);
```

Now if the command `scoreboard wipe` is given, we use the Redis client's `del` function to wipe the key/value pairing by specifying the key.

We also add in some error handling that sends an error message if there are no scores at all:

paul 20:55
scoreboard wipe

awesomebot BOT 20:55
The scoreboard has been wiped!

paul 20:55
scoreboard

awesomebot BOT 20:55
No scores yet! Challenge each other with the `roll` command!

Deleting data should be used with caution

> In a real-world example, scoreboards and other sensitive data constructs should only be deleted by a user with admin rights. Remember that you can check whether the command issuer is an admin by checking the `user.is_admin` property.

Simple to-do example

With the basics of Redis covered, we shall now move on to create a simple to-do Slack bot. The aim of this bot is to allow users to create a to-do list, allowing them to add, complete, and delete a task from this list as they go about their day.

This time, we will start with a skeleton of what we want and build each feature step by step. Start by adding this new command to your bot:

```
bot.respondTo('todo', (message, channel, user) => {
  let args = getArgs(message.text);

  switch(args[0]) {
    case 'add':

      break;
```

```
    case 'complete':

      break;

    case 'delete':

      break;

    case 'help':
      channel.send('Create tasks with \`todo add [TASK]\`,
      complete them with \`todo complete [TASK_NUMBER]\` and
      remove them with \`todo delete [TASK_NUMBER]\` or \`todo
      delete all\`');
      break;

    default:
      showTodos(user.name, channel);
      break;
  }
}, true);

function showTodos(name, channel) {
  client.smembers(name, (err, set) => {
    if (err || set.length < 1) {
      channel.send(`You don\'t have any tasks listed yet,
      ${name}!`);
      return;
    }

    channel.send(`${name}'s to-do list:`);

    set.forEach((task, index) => {
      channel.send(`${index + 1}. ${task}`);
    });
  });
}
```

The bot's behavior will change depending on the second command given after the initial `todo` command. In this instance, a `switch` statement is ideal. We allow for five options: `add`, `complete`, `delete`, `help`, and a default option that is triggered when anything else is passed in.

The help and default behaviors have already been completed, as they are fairly straightforward. In the latter's case, we retrieve the Redis set, send out an error if it doesn't exist or has no items and otherwise send the total to-do list.

Display a message if there are no to-dos

Adding a to-do task is simple as well. We are using a Redis set, as we do not want to allow duplicates in our list. To add an item, we use the previously introduced sadd command. To make our switch statement less cluttered, all the code will be moved to a separate function:

```
case 'add':
  addTask(user.name, args.slice(1).join(' '), channel);
    break;
```

And the addTask function:

```
function addTask(name, task, channel) {
  if (task === '') {
    channel.send('Usage: \`todo add [TASK]\`');
    return;
  }

  client.sadd(name, task);
  channel.send('You added a task!');
  showTodos(name, channel);
}
```

All arguments after the first two (todo add) are joined into a single string and added to our set with the user's name as our key. Remember, duplicates are not allowed in a Redis set, so it's safe to store the task without doing any prior checking. We do check to make sure the task argument is not empty, sending a gentle reminder of how to use the "add" function if it is.

After the task is set, we display a confirmation and the entire to-do list. This is behavior that we will implement for every action, as it's a good practice to show the user what they've done and how it's impacted the data.

Here is an example of adding tasks to our to-do list:

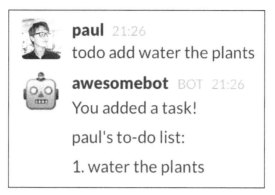

Redis' set takes care of the index for us

Next up is the `complete` command, which takes the number of a task as an argument:

```
case 'complete':
  completeTask(user.name, parseInt(args[1], 10), channel);
  break;
```

Here's the accompanying `completeTask` function:

```
function completeTask(name, taskNum, channel) {
  if (Number.isNaN(taskNum)) {
    channel.send('Usage: \`todo complete [TASK_NUMBER]\`');
    return;
  }

  client.smembers(name, (err, set) => {
    if (err || set.length < 1) {
      channel.send(`You don\'t have any tasks listed yet,
      ${user.name}!`);
      return;
    }

    // make sure no task numbers that are out of bounds are given
    if (taskNum > set.length || taskNum <= 0) {
      channel.send('Oops, that task doesn\'t exist!');
      return;
    }

    let task = set[taskNum - 1];

    if (/~/i.test(task)) {
      channel.send('That task has already been completed!');
      return;
```

```
    }

    // remove the task from the set
    client.srem(name, task);

    // re-add the task, but with a strikethrough effect
    client.sadd(name, `~${task}~`);

    channel.send('You completed a task!');
    showTodos(name, channel);
  });
}
```

This action is a little more complicated, as we have to do a little more error handling to begin with. First, we make sure that the argument provided is a valid number by using the ES6 `Number.isNaN` method.

 Be careful when using ES5's `isNaN` method or ES6's `Number.isNaN` method, as they can be confusing. These methods answer the question *is the value equal to the type NaN? rather than is the value a number?* For more information, visit `https://ponyfoo.com/articles/es6-number-improvements-in-depth#numberisnan`.

After retrieving the set from Redis, we ensure that tasks exist, that the number provided makes sense (for example, not less than 1 or more than the length of the set), and that the task hasn't already been completed. The latter is determined by whether the task has any tilde (~) operators contained within. Messages containing a tilde as the first and last character will render in strikethrough style within Slack.

To complete a task, we remove the task from the Redis set (using `srem`) after assigning it to the `task` variable, and then add it to Redis again with the strikethrough style.

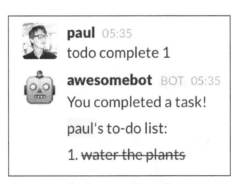

Complete a task by referencing its task number

Finally, let's look at the delete function:

```
case 'delete':
     removeTaskOrTodoList(user.name, args[1], channel);
     break;
```

Here's the accompanying function:

```
function removeTaskOrTodoList(name, target, channel) {
  if (typeof target === 'string' && target === 'all') {
    client.del(name);
    channel.send('To-do list cleared!');
    return;
  }

  let taskNum = parseInt(target, 10);

  if (Number.isNaN(taskNum)) {
    channel.send('Usage: \`todo delete [TASK_NUMBER]\` or \`todo
    delete all\`');
    return;
  }

  // get the set and the exact task
  client.smembers(name, (err, set) => {
    if (err || set.length < 1) {
      channel.send(`You don\'t have any tasks to delete,
      ${name}!`);
      return;
    }

    if (taskNum > set.length || taskNum <= 0) {
      channel.send('Oops, that task doesn\'t exist!');
      return;
    }

    client.srem(name, set[taskNum - 1]);
    channel.send('You deleted a task!');
    showTodos(name, channel);
  });
}
```

The first thing to note in this function is how we use a type of function overloading to achieve two different outcomes, depending on the arguments passed in.

Because JavaScript is a loosely typed language, we can perform actions depending on whether the target argument is a string or a number. In the case of a string (and provided that that string equals *all*), we delete the entire set from Redis using the del command, clearing the whole to-do list.

In case of a number, we only delete the task specified, provided that the target is a valid number we can use (for example, not smaller than 1 and not greater than the length of the set).

Here's the multiple functionality of the `delete` command in action:

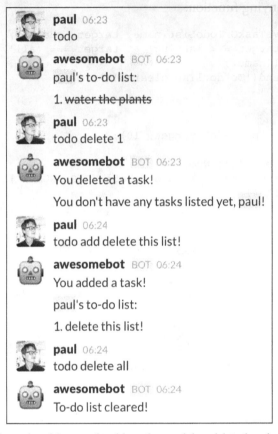

List the to-dos, delete a task, add another, and then delete the whole list

Summary

In this chapter, the reader has learned the basics of the persistent data storage Redis and how to use it through the Node Redis client. We outlined the reasons why Redis lends itself well for use with bots, particularly when keeping a score list or storing multiple small items.

In the next chapter, we will introduce the concept of **natural language processing (NLP)** and see how to evaluate and generate natural language for use in a bot.

5
Understanding and Responding to Natural Language

We've built bots that can play games, store data, and provide useful information. The next step isn't information gathering, it's processing. This chapter will introduce **natural language processing** (**NLP**) and show how we can use it to enhance our bots even further.

In this chapter, we will cover:

- A brief introduction to natural language
- A Node implementation
- Natural language processing
- Natural language generation
- Displaying data in a natural way

A brief introduction to natural language

You should always strive to make your bot as helpful as possible. In all the bots we've made so far, we've awaited clear instructions via a key word from the user and then followed said instructions as far as the bot is capable. What if we could infer instructions from users without them actually providing a key word? Enter **natural language processing** (**NLP**).

NLP can be described as a field of computer science that strives to understand communication and interactions between computers and human (natural) languages.

In layman's terms, NLP is the process of a computer interpreting conversational language and responding by executing a command or replying to the user in an equally conversational tone.

Examples of NLP projects are digital assistants such as the iPhone's Siri. Users can ask questions or give commands and receive answers or confirmation in natural language, seemingly from a human.

One of the more famous projects using NLP is IBM's Watson system. In 2011, Watson famously competed against human opponents in the TV show Jeopardy! and won first place.

The NLP field is a large and complicated one, with many years of research performed by prestigious academic institutions and by large technology companies. Watson alone took 5 years, $3 million, and a small army of academics and engineers to build. In this chapter, the main concepts will briefly be described and a practical example given.

First, let's take a step back and see how NLP might benefit our bots. If we built a bot that retrieves the weather report, we could imagine the command to look something like this:

```
weather amsterdam tomorrow
```

This would return tomorrow's weather report for the city of Amsterdam. What if the bot could retrieve the weather report without requiring a command to be issued? For instance, if a Slack user were to send the message "Will it rain tomorrow?", then the bot would respond with tomorrow's weather report. This is NLP at work; it is the breakdown of natural language into instructions that can be interpreted by the program as a command.

To help us in our understanding of NLP, we will be using a helper library that abstracts the more complicated algorithms away. A good NLP framework is the Python language-based **natural language toolkit** (**NLTK**) available at `http://www.nltk.org/`.

Luckily for us, a project to port the major functions of NLTK to Node has been functioning for some time and has reached a high enough level of maturity for us to use it seamlessly with our existing JavaScript projects. Known as Natural (`https://github.com/NaturalNode/natural`), this library will be our key point of entry to the world of NLP.

Let's start by introducing some of the more common NLP algorithms. Afterwards, we'll use our newfound knowledge by building a simple weather bot, as outlined earlier.

Fundamentals of NLP

NLP, at its core, works by splitting a chunk of text (also referred to as a corpus) into individual segments or tokens and then analyzing them. These tokens might simply be individual words but might also be word contractions. Let's look at how a computer might interpret the phrase: *I have watered the plants.*

If we were to split this corpus into tokens, it would probably look something like this:

```
['I', 'have', 'watered', 'the', 'plants']
```

The word `the` in our corpus is unnecessary as it does not help to understand the phrase's intent— the same for the word `have`. We should therefore remove the surplus words:

```
['I', 'watered', 'plants']
```

Already, this is starting to look more usable. We have a personal pronoun in the form of an actor (`I`), an action or verb (`watered`), and a recipient or noun (`plants`). From this, we can deduce exactly which action is enacted to what and by whom. Furthermore, by conjugating the verb `watered`, we can establish that this action occurred in the past. Consider how the context and meaning of the phrase changes when we make minor changes: *We are watering the plant.*

By using the same process as previously, we get the following:

```
['We', 'watering', 'plant']
```

The meaning of the phrase has dramatically changed: there are multiple actors involved, the action is in the present and the recipient is singular. The challenge of NLP is the ability to analyze such nuances, arrive at a conclusion with a high enough confidence level, and then perform actions based on that conclusion.

A computer, much like a person, learns this nuance by practice and by picking up patterns. A common NLP term is to train your system to recognize context in a corpus. By providing a large amount of predefined phrases to our system, we can analyze said phrases and look for similar ones in other corpus'. We will talk more about how to use this training or classifying technique later.

Let's now look at how we can actually perform the actions explained in the beginning of this section, starting with the splitting of a corpus into a series of tokens, also known as **tokenizing**.

Tokenizers

Start by creating a new project with `npm init`. Name your bot "weatherbot" (or something similar), and install the Slack and Natural APIs with the following command:

```
npm install @slack/client natural –save
```

Copy our `Bot` class from the previous chapters and enter the following in `index.js`:

```javascript
'use strict';

// import the natural library
const natural = require('natural');

const Bot = require('./Bot');

// initalize the tokenizer
const tokenizer = new natural.WordTokenizer();

const bot = new Bot({
  token: process.env.SLACK_TOKEN,
  autoReconnect: true,
  autoMark: true
});

// respond to any message that comes through
bot.respondTo('', (message, channel, user) => {

  let tokenizedMessage = tokenizer.tokenize(message.text);

  bot.send(`Tokenized message: ${JSON.stringify(tokenizedMessage)}`,
channel);
});
```

Start up your Node process and type a test phrase into Slack:

paul 19:36
This is a long sentence, or is it?

weatherbot BOT 19:36
Tokenized message: ["This","is","a","long","sentence","or","is","it"]

The returned tokenized message

Through the use of tokenization, the bot has split the given phrase into short fragments or **tokens**, ignoring punctuation and special characters. Note that we are using the native JSON object's stringify method to convert the JavaScript array into a string before sending it to the channel.

This particular tokenized algorithm will handle contractions (for example, hasn't) by removing the punctuation and splitting the word. Depending on our use case, we might want to use a different algorithm. Luckily, natural provides three different algorithms. Each algorithm returns slightly different results for a corpus. To learn more about these algorithms, visit the natural GitHub page: https://github.com/NaturalNode/natural#tokenizers.

A majority of these algorithms use punctuation (spaces, apostrophes, and so on) to tokenize phrases, whereas the Treebank algorithm analyses contractions (for example, wanna and gimme) to split them into regular words (want to and give me in the case of wanna and gimme). Let's use Treebank for the next example, and replace the line where the tokenizer is initialized with the following:

```
const tokenizer = new natural.TreebankWordTokenizer();
```

Now, return to Slack and try another test message:

paul 19:50
I haven't and cannot

weatherbot BOT 19:50
Tokenized message: ["I","have","n't","and","can","not"]

The Treebank algorithm handles contractions differently

Notice two important things here: the `haven't` contraction was split into two parts, the root verb (`have`) and the contracted add-on (`not`). Furthermore, the word `cannot` was split into two separate words, making the command easier to deal with. This also makes certain slang words like `lemme` and `gotta` easier to process. By splitting the contracted word into two, we can more easily infer whether the phrase is positive or negative. `Can` by itself means positive; however, if it is followed by `not` it changes the context of the phrase to be negative.

Stemmers

Sometimes, it is useful to find the root or `stem` of a word. In the English language, irregular verb conjugations are not uncommon. By deducing the root of a verb, we can dramatically decrease the amount of calculations needed to find the action of the phrase. Take the verb `searching` for example; for the purpose of bots, it would be much easier to process the verb in its root form `search`. Here, a stemmer can help us determine said root. Replace the contents of `index.js` with the following to demonstrate stemmers:

```
'use strict';

// import the natural library
const natural = require('natural');

const Bot = require('./Bot');

// initialize the stemmer
const stemmer = natural.PorterStemmer;

// attach the stemmer to the prototype of String, enabling
// us to use it as a native String function
stemmer.attach();

const bot = new Bot({
  token: process.env.SLACK_TOKEN,
  autoReconnect: true,
  autoMark: true
});

// respond to any message that comes through
bot.respondTo('', (message, channel, user) => {
  let stemmedMessage = stemmer.stem(message.text);

  bot.send(`Stemmed message: ${JSON.stringify(stemmedMessage)}`,
  channel);
});
```

Now, let's see what stemming a word returns:

The conjugated versions of a verb are often different from its root

As expected, `searching` is stemmed into `search` but (more interestingly) the token `shining` is stemmed into `shine`. This shows that the process of stemming is more than simply removing `-ing` from the tail end of a token. Now, we can analyze our tokenized and stemmed corpus and pick out certain verbs or actions. For instance, after stemming, the phrases *I went swimming* and *I swam*, both contain the verb `swim`, which means we only have to search for one term (`swim`) rather than two (`swimming` and `swam`).

Stemming also works for removing plurals from words. For instance, `searches` stems into `search` and `rains` into `rain`.

Let's combine the concepts of tokenizing and stemming into one program to see its effects. Once again, replace `index.js` with the following:

```
'use strict';

// import the natural library
const natural = require('natural');

const Bot = require('./Bot');

// initialize the stemmer
const stemmer = natural.PorterStemmer;

// attach the stemmer to the prototype of String, enabling
```

```
// us to use it as a native String function
stemmer.attach();

const bot = new Bot({
  token: process.env.SLACK_TOKEN,
  autoReconnect: true,
  autoMark: true
});

// respond to any message that comes through
bot.respondTo('', (message, channel, user) => {
  let stemmedMessage = message.text.tokenizeAndStem();

  bot.send(`Tokenize and stemmed message:
  ${JSON.stringify(stemmedMessage)}`, channel);
});
```

Note that we call `tokenizeAndStem` on `message.text`. This might seem odd, until you realize that we have attached the `tokenizeAndStem` method to the `String` object's prototype in earlier code, highlighted in the preceding code.

Switch over to the Slack client and you should see:

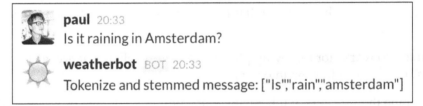

Tokenizing and stemming to produce useful results

The tokenizer and stemming combination has automatically left out very common words such as `it` and `in`, leaving us with a sentence distilled into the most important tokens of the original input.

Using just the tokenized and stemmed result, we can infer that the user wishes to know about the weather in Amsterdam. Furthermore, we can choose to exclude the word `is` from our results. This leaves us with `rain amsterdam`, which is enough information for us to make a weather API call.

String distance

A string distance measuring algorithm is a calculation of how similar two strings are to one another. The strings `smell` and `bell` can be defined as similar, as they share three characters. The strings `bell` and `fell` are even closer, as they share three characters and are only one character apart from one another. When calculating string distance, the string `fell` will receive a higher ranking than `smell` when the distance is measured between them and `bell`.

The NPM package `natural` provides three different algorithms for string distance calculation: Jaro-Winkler, the Dice coefficient, and the Levenshtein distance. Their main differences can be described as follows:

- **Dice coefficient**: This calculates the difference between strings and represents the difference as a value between zero and one. Zero being completely different and one meaning identical.

- **Jaro-Winkler**: This is similar to the Dice Coefficient, but gives greater weighting to similarities at the beginning of the string.

- **Levenshtein distance**: This calculates the amount of edits or steps required to transform one string into another. Zero steps means the strings are identical.

Let's use the Levenshtein distance algorithm to demonstrate its use:

```
let distance = natural.LevenshteinDistance('weather', 'heater');

console.log('Distance:', distance); // distance of 10

let distance2 = natural.LevenshteinDistance('weather', 'weather');

console.log('Distance2:', distance2); // distance of 0
```

A popular use for string distances is to perform a fuzzy search, where the search returns values that are a low string distance from the requested query. String distance calculation can be particularly useful for bots when processing a command with a typo in it. For instance, if a user meant to request the weather report for Amsterdam by sending the command `weather amsterdam`, but instead typed `weater amsterdam`. By calculating the Levenshtein distance between the strings, we can make an educated guess as to the user's intent. Check out the following snippet:

```
bot.respondTo('', (message, channel, user) => {
  // grab the command from the message's text
  let command = message.text.split(' ')[0];
```

```
let distance = natural.LevenshteinDistance('weather', command);

// our typo tolerance, a higher number means a larger
// string distance
let tolerance = 2;

// if the distance between the given command and 'weather' is
// only 2 string distance, then that's considered close enough
if (distance <= tolerance) {
  bot.send(`Looks like you were trying to get the weather,
  ${user.name}!`, channel);
}}, true);
```

Here's the result in Slack:

Calculating string distance can make your bot a lot more user friendly

We set our tolerance to be quite low in this case, allowing for two mistakes or `steps` to indicate a hit. In production code, it would make sense to reduce the tolerance to only one step.

Be careful when choosing which string similarity algorithm to use, as each might determine distance differently. For instance, when using the Jaro-Winkler and Dice Coefficient algorithms, a score of 1 indicates that the two strings are identical. With the Levenshtein difference, it is the opposite, where 0 means identical and the higher the number the larger the string distance.

Inflection

An inflector can be used to convert a noun back and forth from its singular and plural forms. This is useful when generating natural language, as the plural versions of nouns might not be obvious:

```
let inflector = new natural.NounInflector();

console.log(inflector.pluralize('virus'));
console.log(inflector.singularize('octopi'));
```

The preceding code will output `viri` and `octopus`, respectively.

Inflectors may also be used to transform numbers into their ordinal forms; for example, 1 becomes 1st, 2 becomes 2nd, and so on:

```
let inflector = natural.CountInflector;

console.log(inflector.nth(25));
console.log(inflector.nth(42));
console.log(inflector.nth(111));
```

This outputs `25th`, `42nd`, and `111th`, respectively.

Here's an example of the inflector used in a simple bot command:

```
let inflector = natural.CountInflector;

bot.respondTo('what day is it', (message, channel) => {
  let date = new Date();

  // use the ECMAScript Internationalization API to convert
  // month numbers into names
  let locale = 'en-us';
  let month = date.toLocaleString(locale, { month: 'long' });
  bot.send(`It is the ${inflector.nth(date.getDate())} of
  ${month}.`, channel);
}, true);
```

Now when asked what day it is, our bot can respond a little more naturally:

paul 21:51
what day is it

weatherbot BOT 21:51
It is the 28th of March.

Inflection can make your bot more personable

This leads us to our next topic: how to display data in an easy-to-understand way.

Displaying data in a natural way

Let's build our bot's weather functionality. To do this, we will be using a third-party API called **Open Weather Map**. The API is free to use for up to 60 calls per minute, with further pricing options available. To obtain the API key, you will need to sign up here: `https://home.openweathermap.org/users/sign_up`.

Remember that you can pass variables such as API keys into Node from the command line. To run the weather bot, you could use the following command:

`SLACK_TOKEN=[YOUR_SLACK_TOKEN] WEATHER_API_KEY=[YOUR_`
`WEATHER_KEY] nodemon index.js`

Once you signed up and obtained your API key, copy and paste the following code into `index.js`, replacing `process.env.WEATHER_API_KEY` with your newly acquired Open Weather Map key:

```
'use strict';

// import the natural library
const natural = require('natural');

const request = require('superagent');

const Bot = require('./Bot');

const weatherURL =
`http://api.openweathermap.org/data/2.5/weather?&units=metric&appi
d=${process.env.WEATHER_API_KEY}&q=`;
```

```
// initialize the stemmer
const stemmer = natural.PorterStemmer;

// attach the stemmer to the prototype of String, enabling
// us to use it as a native String function
stemmer.attach();

const bot = new Bot({
  token: process.env.SLACK_TOKEN,
  autoReconnect: true,
  autoMark: true
});

bot.respondTo('weather', (message, channel, user) => {
  let args = getArgs(message.text);

  let city = args.join(' ');

  getWeather(city, (error, fullName, description, temperature) => {
    if (error) {
      bot.send(error.message, channel);
      return;
    }

    bot.send(`The weather for ${fullName} is ${description} with a
    temperature of ${Math.round(temperature)} celsius.`, channel);
  });
}, true);

function getWeather(location, callback) {
  // make an AJAX GET call to the Open Weather Map API
  request.get(weatherURL + location)
    .end((err, res) => {
      if (err) throw err;
      let data = JSON.parse(res.text);

      if (data.cod === '404') {
        return callback(new Error('Sorry, I can\'t find that
        location!'));
      }

      console.log(data);

      let weather = [];
```

```
      data.weather.forEach((feature) => {
        weather.push(feature.description);
      });

      let description = weather.join(' and ');

      callback(data.name, description, data.main.temp);
    });
}

// Take the message text and return the arguments
function getArgs(msg) {
  return msg.split(' ').slice(1);
}
```

Using familiar code, our bot performs the following tasks:

- Initializes the stemmer from the natural package and attaches it to the string prototype
- Awaits the `weather` command and uses the `getWeather` function to retrieve the Open Weather Map weather data via an **Asynchronous JavaScript and XML (AJAX)** call
- Sends a formatted weather message to the channel

Here's the bot in action:

paul 19:01
weather new york

weatherbot BOT 19:01
The weather for New York is light rain and thunderstorm with light drizzle with a temperature of 13 celsius.

A simple weatherbot

After receiving the command and the place name, the bot sends an AJAX request to Open Weather Map with the place name as the argument. In return, we get a JSON response that looks like this:

```
{
  coord: { lon: 4.89, lat: 52.37 },
  weather:
   [ { id: 310,
       main: 'Drizzle',
       description: 'light intensity drizzle rain',
       icon: '09n' } ],
  base: 'cmc stations',
```

```
main: { temp: 7, pressure: 1021, humidity: 93, temp_min: 7,
temp_max: 7 },
wind: { speed: 5.1, deg: 340 },
clouds: { all: 75 },
dt: 1458500100,
sys:
  { type: 1,
    id: 5204,
    message: 0.0103,
    country: 'NL',
    sunrise: 1458452421,
    sunset: 1458496543 },
id: 2759794,
name: 'Amsterdam',
cod: 200
}
```

Note how among the plethora of information we get back there is the full, capitalized name of the place and useful information such as minimum and maximum temperature. For our bot's initial purpose, we will use the temperature object (`main`), the `name` property, and the `description` inside the `weather` object.

Now that we have a simple bot which responds to the command `weather`, let's see if we can use NLP to get more specific answers.

Notice how the Open Weather Map AJAX call was abstracted out into the `getWeather` function. This means we can use the same function for both command calls and NLP calls.

Before we continue, we should discuss the right use case for NLP techniques.

When to use NLP?

It might be tempting to have weatherbot listen to and process all messages sent in the channel. This immediately poses some problems:

- How do we know if the message sent is a query on the weather or is completely unrelated?

- Which geographic location is the query about?

- Is the message a question or a statement? For example, the difference between *Is it cold in Amsterdam* and *It is cold in Amsterdam.*

Although an NLP-powered solution to the preceding questions could probably be found, we have to face facts: it's likely that our bot will get at least one of the above points wrong when listening to generic messages. This will lead the bot to either provide bad information or provide unwanted information, thus becoming annoying. If there's one thing we need to avoid at all costs, it's a bot that sends too many wrong messages too often.

Here's an example of a bot using NLP and completely missing the point of the message sent:

paul 22:09
I like to drink my hot tea in bed

weatherbot BOT 22:09
It's currently 16 degrees celsius in Dipayal, that's nice!

A clearly misunderstood message

If a bot were to often mistake your unrelated messages for actual commands, you can imagine users disabling your bot very quickly after enabling it.

The best possible solution would be to create a bot that has human-level natural language processing. If that sentence doesn't concern you, then consider that human-level natural language processing is considered an AI-complete problem. Essentially, it is equivalent to attempting to solve the problem of making computers as intelligent as humans.

Instead, we should focus on how to make our bot perform as best as possible with the resources at hand. We can start by introducing a new rule: use NLP as an enhancement for your bot, not as a main feature.

An example of this is to only use NLP techniques when the bot is directly addressed in a mention. A mention in a Slack channel is when a user sends a message directly to another user in a public channel. This is done by prefacing the user's name with the @ symbol. Bots can also be mentioned, which means we should be able to process the weather command in two ways:

- The user prefaces their request with the command weather: `weather is it raining in Amsterdam`

- The user uses a mention `@weatherbot is it raining in Amsterdam`

Mentions

To implement the second point, we need to revisit our `Bot` class and add mention functionality. In the `Bot` class' constructor, replace the `RTM_CONNECTION_OPENED` event listener block with the following:

```
this.slack.on(CLIENT_EVENTS.RTM.RTM_CONNECTION_OPENED, () => {
  let user = this.slack.dataStore.
  getUserById(this.slack.activeUserId)
  let team = this.slack.dataStore.
  getTeamById(this.slack.activeTeamId);

  this.name = user.name;
  this.id = user.id;

  console.log(`Connected to ${team.name} as ${user.name}`);
});
```

The only change here is the addition of the bot's `id` to the `this` object. This will help us later. Now, replace the `respondTo` function with this:

```
respondTo(opts, callback, start) {
  if (!this.id) {
    // if this.id doesn't exist, wait for slack to connect
    // before continuing
    this.slack.on(CLIENT_EVENTS.RTM.RTM_CONNECTION_OPENED, () => {
      createRegex(this.id, this.keywords);
    });
  } else {
    createRegex(this.id, this.keywords);
  }

  function createRegex(id, keywords) {
    // if opts is an object, treat it as options
    // otherwise treat it as the keywords string
    if (opts === Object(opts)) {
      opts = {
        mention: opts.mention || false,
        keywords: opts.keywords || '',
        start: start || false
      };
    } else {
      opts = {
```

```
        mention: false,
        keywords: opts,
        start: start || false
    };
}


// mention takes priority over start variable
if (opts.mention) {
    // if 'mention' is truthy, make sure the bot only
    // responds to mentions of the bot
    opts.keywords = `<@${id}>:* ${opts.keywords}`;
} else {
    // If 'start' is truthy, prepend the '^' anchor to instruct
    // the expression to look for matches at the beginning of
    // the string
    opts.keywords = start ? '^' + opts.keywords : opts.keywords;
}


// Create a new regular expression, setting the case
// insensitive (i) flag
// Note: avoid using the global (g) flag
let regex = new RegExp(opts.keywords, 'i');


// Set the regular expression to be the key, with the callback
// function as the value
keywords.set(regex, callback);
    }
}
```

We've improved the `respondTo` function by first checking whether `this.id` exists. If not, it means that we've not yet successfully connected to Slack. Therefore, we wait till Slack has connected (remember how we set `this.id` in the constructor after connecting) and then proceed. This is the second time we listen for the `RTM_CONNECTION_OPENED` event. Luckily, the first time it happens in the `Bot` class' constructor, which means this listener will always trigger second as it was added later. This ensures that `this.id` is defined once the event triggers.

The function now takes either a string (the keywords we're looking for) or an object as its first parameter. In the case of an object, we check to see whether the mention property is truthy; if so, we create a regular expression that purposefully looks for the mention syntax. When a message is received, a mention takes the following structure:

```
<@[USER_ID]>: [REST OF MESSAGE]
```

Switch back to `index.js` and let's try out our new code by replacing the previous `respondTo` block of `weather`:

```
bot.respondTo({ mention: true }, (message, channel, user) => {
  let args = getArgs(message.text);

  let city = args.join(' ');

  getWeather(city, (error, fullName, description, temperature) =>
  {
    if (error) {
      bot.send(error.message, channel);
      return;
    }

    bot.send(`The weather for ${fullName} is ${description} with a
    temperature of ${Math.round(temperature)} celsius.`, channel);
  });
});
```

Now when we mention our bot and pass a city name, we get the following result:

paul 14:50
@weatherbot: amsterdam

weatherbot BOT 14:50
The weather for Amsterdam is broken clouds with a temperature of 6 celsius.

Mentions can be used to identify specific behavior

Mentions are a great way to ensure that the message sent is meant to be a command for your bot. When implementing a natural language solution, it is highly recommended you use mentions.

Now with mentions in place, let's look at how we're going to answer weather-related questions in an NLP way. We briefly talked about classification and the training of NLP systems earlier. Let's revisit that topic and see how we can use it for our weather bot.

Classifiers

Classification is the process of training your bot to recognize a phrase or pattern of words and to associate them with an identifier. To do this, we use a classification system built into `natural`. Let's start with a small example:

```
const classifier = new natural.BayesClassifier();

classifier.addDocument('is it hot', ['temperature',
'question','hot']);
classifier.addDocument('is it cold', ['temperature', 'question'
'cold']);
classifier.addDocument('will it rain today', ['conditions',
'question', 'rain']);
classifier.addDocument('is it drizzling', ['conditions',
'question', 'rain']);

classifier.train();


console.log(classifier.classify('will it drizzle today'));
console.log(classifier.classify('will it be cold out'));
```

The first log prints:

```
conditions,question,rain
```

The second log prints:

```
temperature,question,cold
```

The classifier stems the string to be classified first, and then calculates which of the trained phrases it is the most similar to by assigning a weighting to each possibility.

You can view the weightings by using the following code:

```
console.log(classifier.getClassifications('will it drizzle
today'));
```

The output is as follows:

```
[ { label: 'conditions,question,rain',
    value: 0.17777777777777773 },
  { label: 'temperature,question,hot', value: 0.05 },
  { label: 'temperature,question,cold', value: 0.05 } ]
```

To get accurate and reliable results, you must train your bot with potentially hundreds of phrases. Luckily, you can also import training data JSON files into the classifier.

Save your classifier training data by creating a `classifier.json` file in your directory:

```
classifier.save('classifier.json', (err, classifier) => {
  // the classifier is saved to the classifier.json file!
});
```

Retrieve the same file with the following code:

```
natural.BayesClassifier.load('classifier.json', null, (err,
classifier) => {
  if (err) {
    throw err;
  }

  console.log(classifier.classify('will it drizzle today'));
});
```

Now let's try and use classifiers to power our weatherbot.

Using trained classifiers

An example `classifier.json` file that contains training data for weather is included with this book. For the rest of this chapter, we will assume that the file is present and that we are loading it in via the preceding method.

Replace your `respondTo` method call with the following snippet:

```
let settings = {};

bot.respondTo({ mention: true }, (message, channel, user) => {
  let args = getArgs(message.text);

  if (args[0] === 'set') {
    let place = args.slice(1).join(' ');
    settings[user.name] = place

    bot.send(`Okay ${user.name}, I've set ${place} as your default
    location`, channel);
    return;
  }
```

```
if (args.indexOf('in') < 0 && !settings[user.name]) {
  bot.send(`Looks like you didn\'t specify a place name, you can
  set a city by sending \`@weatherbot set [city name]\` or by
  sending \`@weatherbot ${args.join(' ')} in [city name]\``,
  channel);
  return;
}


// The city is usually preceded by the word 'in'
let city = args.indexOf('in') > 0 ?
args.slice(args.indexOf('in') + 1) : settings[user.name];


let option = classifier.classify(message.text).split(',');


console.log(option);


// Set the typing indicator as we're doing an asynchronous
request
bot.setTypingIndicator(channel);


getWeather(city, (error, fullName, description, temperature) =>
{
  if (error) {
    bot.send(`Oops, an error occurred, please try again later!`,
    channel);
    return;
  }

  let response = '';

  switch(option[0]) {
    case 'weather':
      response = `It is currently ${description} with a
      temperature of ${Math.round(temperature)} celsius in
      ${fullName}.`;
      break;

    case 'conditions':
      response = `${fullName} is experiencing ${description}
      right now.`;
      break;

    case 'temperature':
      let temp = Math.round(temperature);
```

```
    let flavorText = temp > 25 ? 'hot!' : (temp < 10 ? 'cold!'
    : 'nice!');

    response = `It's currently ${temp} degrees celsius in
    ${fullName}, that's ${flavorText}`;
  }

  bot.send(response, channel);
 });
});
```

Run the Node process and ask weatherbot a series of natural language questions:

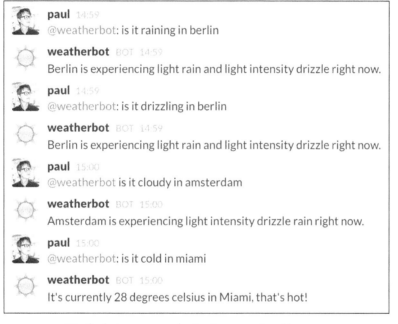

Weatherbot can now understand conversational language

Let's look at the code and see what's going on:

```
let settings = {};

bot.respondTo({ mention: true }, (message, channel, user) => {
  let args = getArgs(message.text);

  if (args[0] === 'set') {
    let place = args.slice(1).join(' ');
    settings[user.name] = place
```

```
bot.send(`Okay ${user.name}, I've set ${place} as your default
location`, channel);
    return;
}
```

First, we check to see whether the keyword `set` is used immediately after the `@weatherbot` mention. If yes, this sets the following arguments to be the default city of the user. We use a simple settings object here, but this could be improved by using a data store such as Redis, explained in *Chapter 4, Using Data*.

You can see an example of the `set` behavior in the following screenshot:

Setting a city saves users from having to type in their place name for each query

Next, we attempt to find the place we want to get weather information for:

```
if (args.indexOf('in') < 0 && !settings[user.name]) {
    bot.send(`Looks like you didn\'t specify a place name, you can
    set a city by sending \`@weatherbot set [city name]\` or by
    sending \`@weatherbot ${args.join(' ')} in [city name]\``,
    channel);
    return;
}

// The city is usually preceded by the word 'in'
let city = args.indexOf('in') > 0 ?
args.slice(args.indexOf('in') + 1) : settings[user.name];
```

We expect all weather queries with a place name to follow the pattern `[condition]` `in` `[place name]`. This means we can make a reasonable assumption that all tokens after the word `in` are the place name to use in our AJAX call.

If the word `in` does not appear and there is no set place name, then we send back an error message with a best guess example of how to use weatherbot.

This is, of course, not the most ideal way to detect a place name – determining which part of the phrase is a place name is notoriously difficult, especially when the name in question comprises multiple words like New York or Dar es Salaam. One possible solution would be to train our bot with a series of city name classifiers (essentially one training phrase per city). Other solutions include the Query GeoParser http://www2009.eprints.org/239/ and the Stanford Named Entity Recognizer http://nlp.stanford.edu/software/CRF-NER.shtml.

Next we use the classifier to identify which key words the message should be associated with:

```
let option = classifier.classify(message.text).split(',');

    console.log(option);

    // Set the typing indicator as we're doing an
    // asynchronous request
    bot.setTypingIndicator(channel);
```

Some of the classifier's phrases are added with an array as the second argument, for example:

```
classifier.addDocument('is it hot outside', ['temperature',
'question', 'hot']);
```

This means that the returned value from the classifier.classify method is a comma-separated string value. We transform it into a JavaScript array by using the Array.split method.

Finally, we set the typing indicator, which is good practice when making an asynchronous call:

```
getWeather(city, (error, fullName, description, temperature) => {
    if (error) {
        bot.send(`Oops, an error occurred, please try again later!`,
        channel);
        return;
    }

    let response = '';

    switch(option[0]) {
      case 'weather':
        response = `It is currently ${description} with a
        temperature of ${Math.round(temperature)} celsius in
        ${fullName}.`;
```

```
        break;

    case 'conditions':
        response = `${fullName} is experiencing ${description}
        right now.`;
        break;

    case 'temperature':
        let temp = Math.round(temperature);
        let flavorText = temp > 25 ? 'hot!' : (temp < 10 ? 'cold!'
        : 'nice!');

        response = `It's currently ${temp} degrees celsius in
        ${fullName}, that's ${flavorText}`;
    }

    bot.send(response, channel);
    });
});
```

The value at index 0 of the option object is the state of the question, in this case whether the message is related to the temperature, condition, or generic weather.

Our options are as follows:

- **Temperature**: Send the temperature (in Celsius) to the channel
- **Conditions**: Send the weather conditions (for example, raining and windy) to the channel
- **Weather**: Send both the conditions and temperature to the channel

It is important to understand the underlying concepts of classification and training to build a smarter bot. It is, however, possible to abstract the problem of obtaining training data by using the third-party service wit.ai (`https://wit.ai/`). wit.ai is a free service, created by Facebook, which allows you to train phrases (referred to as **entities** by wit.ai) and to retrieve analysis on a given phrase easily and quickly via an AJAX request.

Alternatively, you could use services such as api.ai (`https://api.ai/`) or Microsoft's LUIS (`https://www.luis.ai/`). Bear in mind, however, that although these services are free and easy to use, it is not guaranteed that they will be free or even around in the future. Unless you are attempting to build something that requires extremely accurate NLP services, it is almost always better to create your own implementation with open source NLP libraries. This has the added benefit of controlling and owning your own data, something which is not guaranteed when using a third-party service.

Now that we know how to process language, we should take a look at how to transform our data into human understandable natural language.

Natural language generation

Natural language can be defined as a conversational tone in a bot's response. The purpose here is not to hide the fact that the bot is not human, but to make the information easier to digest.

The `flavorText` variable from the previous snippet is an attempt to make the bot's responses sound more natural; in addition, it is a useful technique to cheat our way out of performing more complex processing to reach a conversational tone in our response.

Take the following example:

paul 15:46
@weatherbot set new york

weatherbot BOT 15:46
Okay paul, I've set new york as your default location

paul 15:46
@weatherbot is it cold

weatherbot BOT 15:46
It's currently 4 degrees celsius in New York, that's cold!

paul 15:48
@weatherbot temperature in london

weatherbot BOT 15:48
It's currently 8 degrees celsius in London, that's cold!

Weatherbot's politician-like response

Notice how the first weather query is asking whether it's cold or not. Weatherbot gets around giving a yes or no answer by making a generic statement on the temperature to every question.

This might seem like a cheat, but it is important to remember a very important aspect of NLP. *The more complex the generated language, the more likely it is to go wrong.* Generic answers are better than outright wrong answers.

This particular problem could be solved by adding more keywords to our classifiers and adding more phrases. Currently, our `classifier.json` file contains 50 phrases related to the weather; adding more phrases could get us a clearer idea of what is being asked of weatherbot.

This leads us to a very important point in the pursuit of natural language generation.

When should we use natural language generation?

Sparingly, is the answer. Consider Slackbot, Slack's own in-house bot used for setting up new users, amongst other things. Here's the first thing Slackbot says to a new user:

 slackbot 15:38
Hello, I'm Slackbot. I try to be helpful. (But I'm still just a bot. Sorry!) Type **something** to get started.

The humble bot

Immediately, the bot's restrictions are outlined and no attempts to hide the fact that it is not human are made. Natural language generation is at its best when used to transform data-intensive constructs such as JSON objects into easy to comprehend phrases.

The Turing Test is a famous test developed in 1950 by Alan Turing to assess a machine's ability to make itself indistinguishable from a human in a text-only sense. Like Slackbot, you should not strive to make your bot Turing Test complete. Instead, focus on how your bot can be the most useful and use natural language generation to make your bot as easy to use as possible.

The uncanny valley

The uncanny valley is a term used to describe systems that act and sound like humans, but are somehow slightly off. This slight discrepancy actually leads to the bot feeling a lot more unnatural, and this is the exact opposite of what we are trying to accomplish with natural language generation. Instead, we should avoid trying to make the bot perfect in its natural language responses; the chances of finding ourselves in the uncanny valley get higher the more human-like we try to make a bot sound.

Instead, we should focus on making our bots useful and easy to use, over making its responses natural. A good principle to follow is to build your bot to *be as smart as a puppy*, a concept championed by Matt Jones (http://berglondon.com/blog/2010/09/04/b-a-s-a-a-p/):

> *"Making smart things that don't try to be too smart and fail, and indeed, by design, make endearing failures in their attempts to learn and improve. Like puppies."*

Let's expand our weatherbot to make the generated response sound a little more natural (but not too natural).

First, edit the `getWeather` function to include `data` as a final argument in its callback call:

```
callback(null, data.name, condition, data.main.temp, data);
```

Then add the `data` variable to the callback we assign in the mention `respondsTo`:

```
getWeather(city, (error, fullName, description, temperature, data)
=> {
```

In the `switch` statement within the `getWeather` call, replace the `weather` case with this:

```
case 'weather':
        // rain is an optional variable
        let rain = data.rain ? `Rainfall in the last 3 hours has
        been ${data.rain['3h']} mm.` : ''

        let expression = data.clouds.all > 80 ? 'overcast' :
        (data.clouds.all < 25 ? 'almost completely clear' :
        'patchy');
        // in case of 0 cloud cover
        expression = data.clouds.all === 0 ? 'clear skies' :
        expression;

        let clouds = `It's ${expression} with a cloud cover of
        ${data.clouds.all}%.`;

        response = `It is currently ${description} with a
        temperature of ${Math.round(temperature)} celsius in
        ${fullName}. The predicted high for today is
        ${Math.round(data.main.temp_max)} with a low of
        ${Math.round(data.main.temp_min)} celsius and
        ${data.main.humidity}% humidity. ${clouds} ${rain}`;
        break;
```

Asking for the weather in a city will now instruct our bot to send this:

paul 18:25
@weatherbot what's the weather like in manilla

weatherbot BOT 18:25
It is currently overcast clouds with a temperature of 20 celsius in Manilla. The predicted high for today is 20 with a low of 20 celsius and 56% humidity. It's overcast with a cloud cover of 90%. Rainfall in the last 3 hours has been 0.72 mm.

paul 18:25
@weatherbot how's the weather in hyderabad

weatherbot BOT 18:25
It is currently clear sky with a temperature of 23 celsius in Hyderabad. The predicted high for today is 23 with a low of 23 celsius and 45% humidity. It's clear skies with a cloud cover of 0%.

Weatherbot can now be a bit more specific with its reporting

Here, we've simply taken the JSON returned from the AJAX call and formatted the data into something a bit more legible by humans. Rainfall is included, but only if there actually was any in the last 3 hours (if not, the `rain` property is omitted from the returned data). Cloud cover is represented by a percentage, which is perfect for us as we can assign predetermined statements (`patchy`, `almost completely clear` and `clear skies`) depending on that percentage.

When generating natural language, think of how your data can be presented. Percentages are an excellent way of assigning a verbal value. For example, anything between 80 and 100 percent can use adverbs like `extremely` or `very`, whereas we can use `barely` and `very little` for 0 to 20 percent.

For some data sets, a paragraph might be easier to digest rather than a list or pure data.

The result is a bot that, in a conversational tone, can give a weatherman-like weather report on the area in question.

Summary

In this chapter, we discussed what NLP is and how it can be leveraged to make a bot seem far more complex than it really is. By using these techniques, natural language can be read, processed, and responded to in equally natural tones. We also covered the limitations of NLP and understood how to differentiate between good and bad uses of NLP.

In the next chapter, we will explore the creation of web-based bots, which can interact with Slack using webhooks and slash commands.

6
Webhooks and Slash Commands

Every bot we've created so far shares the same two traits: they rely on commands issued by users and require a Slack API token. This has been very useful in our bots so far, but what if we want a bot to post messages to a Slack channel without needing an API token? Plus what if we want a bot that does not require an API token to interact with users? An example of this is the GitHub Slack integration, a service that posts GitHub activity on specific repositories to a Slack channel of your choice.

In this chapter, we will discuss how to use webhooks to get data in and out of Slack and how to create slash commands that users can interact with throughout Slack.

We will cover the following topics:

- Webhooks
- Incoming webhooks
- Outgoing webhooks
- Slash commands
- In-channel and ephemeral responses

Webhooks

A webhook is a way of altering or augmenting a web application through HTTP methods. Previously, we used third-party APIs in our bots to get data into and out of Slack. However, this isn't the only way. Webhooks allow us to post message to and from Slack using regular HTTP requests with a JSON payload. What makes a webhook a bot is its ability to post messages to Slack as if they are a bot user.

These webhooks can be divided into incoming and outgoing webhooks, each with their own purposes and uses.

Incoming webhooks

An example of an incoming webhook would be a service that relays information from an external source to a Slack channel without being explicitly requested. An example of this is the aforementioned GitHub Slack integration:

github BOT 15:07

[vendor-management-tool] New branch "paul/ship-to-customer" was pushed by PaulAsjes

The GitHub integration posts messages about repositories we are interested in

In the preceding screenshot, we can see how a message was sent to Slack after a new branch was made on a repository this team is watching. This data wasn't explicitly requested by a team member, but it was automatically sent to the channel as a result of the incoming webhook.

Other popular examples include a Jenkins integration, where infrastructure changes can be monitored in Slack (for example, if a server watched by Jenkins goes down, a warning message can be posted immediately to a relevant Slack channel).

Let's start by setting up an incoming webhook that sends a simple *Hello world* message:

1. First, navigate to the Custom Integration Slack team page (`https://my.slack.com/apps/build/custom-integration`).

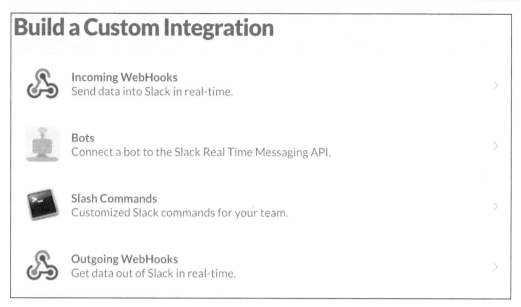

The various flavors of custom integration

2. Select **Incoming WebHooks** from the list, and then select the channel you'd like your webhook app to post messages to:

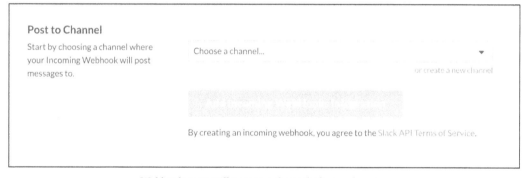

Webhook apps will post to a channel of your choosing

Custom webhooks (that is, webhooks created for your team only) use the selected channel as a default channel to send message to. It is possible to use the same webhook to post to different channels, as we'll see in a moment.

3. Once you've clicked on the **Add Incoming WebHooks integration** button, you will be presented with an options page that allows you to customize your integration a little further.

Descriptive Label
Use this label to provide extra context in your list of integrations (optional).

Optional description of this integration

Customize Name
Choose the username that this integration will post as.

webhook-bot

Customize Icon
Change the icon that is used for messages from this integration.

Upload an image   or   Choose an emoji   Use default icon

Save Settings

Names, descriptions, and icons can be set from this menu

4. Set a customized icon for your integration (for this example, the wave emoji was used) and copy down the webhook URL, which has the following format:

```
https://hooks.slack.com/services/T00000000/B00000000/
XXXXXXXXXXXXXXXXXXXXXXXX
```

This generated URL is unique to your team, meaning that any JSON payloads sent via this URL will only appear in your team's Slack channels.

Now, let's throw together a quick test of our incoming webhook in Node. Start a new Node project (remember you can use npm init to create your package.json) and install the familiar superagent AJAX library by running the following in your terminal:

```
npm install superagent -save
```

Create a file named index.js and paste the following JavaScript code within it:

```
const WEBHOOK_URL = [YOUR_WEBHOOK_URL];

const request = require('superagent');
```

```
request
  .post(WEBHOOK_URL)
  .send({
    text: 'Hello! I am an incoming Webhook bot!'
  })
  .end((err, res) => {
    console.log(res);
  });
```

Remember to replace [YOUR_WEBHOOK_URL] with your newly generated URL, and then run the program by executing the following command:

nodemon index.js

Two things should happen now: firstly a long response should be logged in your terminal and secondly you should see a message like the following in the Slack client:

webhook-bot BOT 22:37

Hello! I am an incoming Webhook bot!

The incoming webhook equivalent of "hello world"

The res object that we logged in our terminal is the response from the AJAX request. Taking the form of a large JavaScript object, it displays information about the HTTP POST request we made to our webhook URL.

Looking at the message received in the Slack client, notice how the name and icon are the same as what we set in our integration setup in the team admin site. Remember that the default icon, name, and channel are used if none are provided, so let's see what happens when we change that around. Replace your request AJAX call in index.js with the following:

```
request
  .post(WEBHOOK_URL)
  .send({
    username: "Incoming bot",
    channel: "#general",
    icon_emoji: ":+1:",
    text: 'Hello! I am different from the previous bot!'
  })
  .end((err, res) => {
    console.log(res);
  });
```

Save the file and `nodemon` will automatically restart the program. Switch over to the Slack client and you should see a message like the following pop up in your `#general` channel:

Incoming bot BOT 21:06

Hello! I am different from the previous bot!

New name, icon, and message

 In place of `icon_emoji`, you could also use `icon_url` to link to a specific image of your choosing.

If you wish your message to only be sent to one user, you can supply a username as the value for the `channel` property:

```
channel: "@paul"
```

This will cause the message to be sent from within the Slackbot direct message. The message's icon and username will match what you either configured in the setup or set in the body of the POST request.

Finally, let's look at sending links in our integration; replace the `text` property with the following and save `index.js`:

```
text: 'Hello! Here is a fun link: <http://www.github.com|Github is great!>'
```

Slack will automatically parse any links it finds, whether it's in the format `http://www.example.com` or `www.example.com`. By enclosing the URL in angled brackets and using the | character, we can specify what we would like the URL to be shown as:

Incoming bot BOT 21:22

Hello! Here is a fun link: Github is great!

Formatted links are easier to read than long URLs

For more information on message formatting, visit `https://api.slack.com/docs/formatting`.

Note that as this is a custom webhook integration, we can change the name, icon, and channel of the integration. If we were to package the integration as a Slack app (an app which is installable by other teams), then it is not possible to override the default channel, username, and icon set.

Incoming webhooks are triggered by external sources—an example would be if a new user signs up to your service or if a product is sold. The goal of the incoming webhook is to provide easy-to-reach and comprehensible information for your team. The opposite would be if you want users to get data out of Slack, which can be done via the medium of outgoing webhooks.

Outgoing webhooks

Outgoing webhooks differ from the incoming variety in that they send data out of Slack and to a service of your choosing, which in turn can respond with a message to the Slack channel.

To set up an outgoing webhook, visit the custom integration page of your Slack team's admin page again (`https://my.slack.com/apps/build/custom-integration`). This time, select the **Outgoing WebHooks** option.

In the next screen, be sure to select a channel, a name, and an icon. Notice how there is a `target` URL field to be filled in; we will fill this out shortly.

When an outgoing webhook is triggered in Slack, an HTTP POST request is made to the URL (or URLs, as you can specify multiples) you provide. So first we need to build a server that can accept our webhook.

In `index.js`, paste the following code:

```
'use strict';
const http = require('http');
// create a simple server with node's built in http module
http.createServer((req, res) => {
  res.writeHead(200, {'Content-Type': 'text/plain'});

  // get the data embedded in the POST request
  req.on('data', (chunk) => {
    // chunk is a buffer, so first convert it to
    // a string and split it to make it more legible as an array
    console.log('Body:', chunk.toString().split('&'));
```

```
  });

  // create a response
  let response = JSON.stringify({
    text: 'Outgoing webhook received!'
  });

  // send the response to Slack as a message
  res.end(response);
}).listen(8080, '0.0.0.0');

console.log('Server running at http://0.0.0.0:8080/');
```

 Notice how we require the http module, despite not installing it with NPM. That is because the http module is a core Node dependency and is automatically included with your installation of Node.

In this block of code, we start a simple server on port 8080 and listen for incoming requests.

In this example, we set our server to run at 0.0.0.0 rather than localhost. This is important as Slack is sending a request to our server, so it needs to be accessible from the Internet. Setting the **Internet Protocol (IP)** of our server to 0.0.0.0 tells Node to use your computer's network-assigned IP address. Therefore, by setting the IP of our server to 0.0.0.0, Slack can reach your server by hitting your IP on port 8080 (for example, http://123.456.78.90:8080).

 If you are having trouble with Slack reaching your server, it is most likely because you are behind a router or firewall. To circumvent this issue, you can use a service such as ngrok (https://ngrok.com/). Alternatively, look into the **Port Forwarding** settings for your router or firewall.

Let's update our outgoing webhook settings accordingly:

The outgoing webhook settings, with destination URL

Save your settings and run your Node app; test that the outgoing webhook works by typing a message into the channel you specified in the webhook's settings. You should then see something like this in Slack:

We built a spam bot

Well the good news is that our server is receiving requests and returning a message to send to Slack. The issue here is that we skipped over the **Trigger Word(s)** field in the webhook settings page. Without a trigger word, any message sent to the specified channel will trigger the outgoing webhook. This causes our webhook to trigger on a message sent by the outgoing webhook in the first place, creating an infinite loop.

To fix this we could do one of two things:

- Refrain from returning a message to the channel when listening to all the channel's messages
- Specify a trigger word or trigger words to ensure we don't spam the channel

Returning a message is optional, yet it is encouraged to ensure a better user experience. Even a confirmation message such as **Message received!** is better than no message, as it confirms to the user that their message was received and is being processed.

Let's presume we prefer the second option and add a trigger word:

Trigger Word(s)   webhook

Trigger words keep our webhooks organized

Now, let's try that again, this time sending a message with the trigger word at the beginning of the message. Restart your Node app and send a new message:

paul 21:49
webhook hi bot!

outgoing-webhook BOT 21:49
Outgoing webhook received!

Our outgoing webhook app now functions a lot like our bots from earlier

Great, now switch over to your terminal and see what that message logged:

```
Body: [ 'token=KJcfN8xakBegb5RReelRKJng',
  'team_id=T000001',
  'team_domain=buildingbots',
  'service_id=34210109492',
  'channel_id=C0J4E5SG6',
  'channel_name=bot-test',
  'timestamp=1460684994.000598',
  'user_id=U0HKKH1TR',
```

```
    'user_name=paul',
    'text=webhook+hi+bot%21',
    'trigger_word=webhook' ]
```

This array contains the body of the HTTP POST request sent by Slack. In it, we have some useful data such as the user's name, the message sent, and the team ID. We can use this data to customize the response or to perform some validation to make sure the user is authorized to use this webhook.

In our response, we simply sent back a **Message received** string. However, like with incoming webhooks, we can set our own username and icon. The channel cannot be different from the channel specified in the webhook's settings. The same restrictions apply when the webhook is not a custom integration. This means that if the webhook was installed as a Slack app for another team, the webhook can only post messages as the username and icon specified in the setup screen. We will cover Slack apps in detail in *Chapter 7, Publishing Your App*.

An important thing to note is that webhooks, either incoming or outgoing, can only be set up in public channels. This is predominantly to discourage abuse and uphold privacy, as we've seen that it's trivial to set up a webhook that can record all the activity in a channel.

If you want similar functionality in private groups or DMs, we can use a slash command instead.

Slash commands

Commands that begin with a slash (/) are commands that can be used from anywhere within the Slack client. You are probably already familiar with the more common ones implemented by Slack themselves. For instance, use the `topic` command:

```
    /topic Sloths are great
```

This will set the channel's topic to "Sloths are great." Like with incoming and outgoing webhooks, Slack allows teams to configure their own custom slash commands. To demonstrate their use, we'll build a bot that uses the popular computational knowledge engine Wolfram Alpha (`http://www.wolframalpha.com/`). The end goal is a bot that returns the results from the query submitted via the slash command.

Unlike webhooks, slash commands can only send data included with the command, so you are guaranteed to only receive data that was intentionally sent. Because of this nuance, we get an additional benefit to using slash commands. They are available to be used from any channel, DM, or private group.

First, let's set up the slash command integration and get a Wolfram Alpha API key. Although we don't specifically need a Slack token, we do require one to access Wolfram Alpha's services. Navigate to your team's integration settings (`https://buildingbots.slack.com/apps/manage/custom-integrations`), select **Slash Commands**, and then select **Add Configuration**. We're going to use the `wolfram` string as our slash command, so let's fill that in and continue.

Choose a Command	/wolfram

The slash command must be unique to your team

Now, specify a URL that the slash command will send a request to, similar to what we did earlier with webhooks.

The slash command can be customized in a different way to webhooks

We have the choice of which HTTP method to use when requesting the provided URL. If you wish to send data to a server, use the **POST** method. If you wish to retrieve data without sending anything, use the **GET** method. For our Wolfram Alpha bot, we will be using **POST**, as we're sending a query to the server we created earlier.

Take special note of the generated token. This is a unique identifier that you can use to ensure that all requests coming to your server are from this particular Slack slash command, allowing you to reject any unwanted requests. We'll get back to the token later.

Next, we will fill out the autocomplete details. Although optional, it is strongly recommended that you fill them out anyway, as they give clear instructions for your users on how to use your slash command.

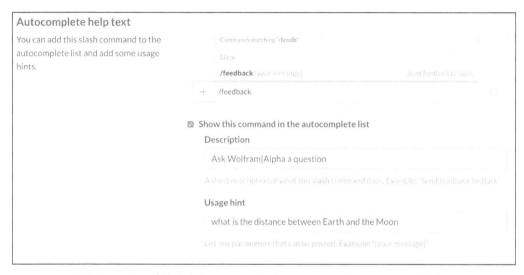

Help text is incredibly helpful to users who have never used your command before

Similar to other third-party APIs we've used in this book, the Wolfram Alpha API requires an API token to access their computational services. To get one, navigate to the following URL and follow the on-screen sign up instructions: `https://developer.wolframalpha.com/portal/apisignup.html`.

Note that the Wolfram Alpha API is only free up to 2000 requests per month. If your slash command exceeds that amount, your requests will be denied unless you pay for a higher-tier service.

The Wolfram Alpha API sends responses in XML, which we'll need to convert to JSON for easier use. Luckily, there is an NPM package that can abstract this problem away for us: `node-wolfram` (`https://www.npmjs.com/package/node-wolfram`). Install the `node-wolfram` package by running the following command:

```
npm install node-wolfram -save
```

Once you have your key and you've installed `node-wolfram`, paste the following code in `index.js`:

```
'use strict';

const http = require('http');
const request = require('superagent');

const WOLFRAM_TOKEN = [YOUR_WOLFRAM_API_TOKEN];
const SLACK_TOKEN = [YOUR_SLACK_TOKEN];

const Client = require('node-wolfram');
const wolfram = new Client(WOLFRAM_TOKEN);

// create a simple server with node's built in http module
http.createServer((req, res) => {
    res.writeHead(200, {'Content-Type': 'text/plain'});

    // get the data embedded in the POST request
    req.on('data', (chunk) => {
      // chunk is a buffer, so first convert it
      // to a string and split it to make it legible
      console.log('Body:', chunk.toString().split('&'));

      let bodyArray = chunk.toString().split('&');
      let bodyObject = {};

      // convert the data array to an object
      for (let i = 0; i < bodyArray.length; i++) {
        // convert the strings into key value pairs
        let arr = bodyArray[i].split('=');
        bodyObject[arr[0]] = arr[1];
      }

      // if the token doesn't match ours, abort
      if (bodyObject.token !== SLACK_TOKEN) {
        return res.end('Invalid token');
      }

      queryWolfram(bodyObject.text.split('+').join(' '), (err,
      result) => {
        if (err) {
          console.log(err);
          return;
```

```
          }

            // send back the result to Slack
            res.end(result);
          });
        });
    }).listen(8080, '0.0.0.0');

console.log('Server running at http://0.0.0.0:8080/');

// make sure to unescape the value so we don't get Unicode
let query = unescape(bodyObject.text.split('+').join(' '));

queryWolfram(query, (err, result) => {   wolfram.query(message,
(err, result) => {
      if (err) {
        return done(err);
      }

      // if the query didn't fail, but the message wasn't understood
      // then send a generic error message
      if (result.queryresult.$.success === 'false') {
        return done(null, 'Sorry, something went wrong, please try
        again');
      }
      let msg = '';

      for (let i = 0; i < result.queryresult.pod.length; i++) {
        let pod = result.queryresult.pod[i];
        msg += pod.$.title + ': \n';

        for (let j = 0; j < pod.subpod.length; j++) {
          let subpod = pod.subpod[j];

          for (let k = 0; k <subpod.plaintext.length; k++) {
            let text = subpod.plaintext[k];
            msg += '\t' + text + '\n';
          }
        }
      }

    done(null, msg);
  });
}
```

Simply put, this block of code listens for incoming requests at port 8080. Once data is received (via a POST request), we convert the data to a JavaScript object for easy use. If the token sent in the request matches the one hardcoded in our program, we send a request to Wolfram Alpha that includes the slash command's content. Luckily, Wolfram Alpha run their own **natural language processing (NLP)**, so we can just send the user's input and let Wolfram Alpha do the heavy lifting. Once we receive a callback from the Wolfram Alpha API, we return the results to Slack, which posts it in the Slack channel. Run your server and type the following command into Slack to see it in action:

```
/wolfram 2 x 2
```

After a few moments, you should see the result:

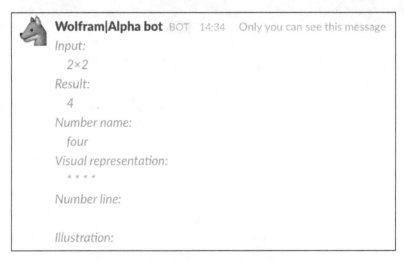

Wolfram Alpha calculates a simple math problem

Success! Now let's try a more challenging query:

```
/wolfram distance between earth and moon
```

That request should result in something like this:

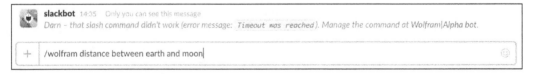

The query took too long

Oh dear, it looks like our query timed out. Were we to add some logging to our app, we'd see that although the Wolfram Alpha API does eventually return a result, it takes more than the maximum timeout period of Slack webhook integrations (3,000 milliseconds). This causes the slash command to fail and displays the preceding error message.

To solve this, let's look at the data received from Slack initially; the body from the previous slash command looks like this:

```
Body: [ 'token=86oxKgPrkxrvPHpmleaP8Rbs',
  'team_id=T00000000',
  'team_domain=buildingbots',
  'channel_id=C0J4E5SG6',
  'channel_name=bot-test',
  'user_id=U0HKKH1TR',
  'user_name=paul',
  'command=%2Fwolfram',
  'text=distance+between+earth+and+moon',
  'response_url=https%3A%2F%2Fhooks.slack.com%2Fcommands
%2FT0HKKH1T9%2F35399194752%2Fm9mIVSHYjMdnwXWyCTYYTIZj' ]
```

The last index of the `Body` array is what interests us—a response URL. Should your calculations take longer than the maximum timeout of 3000 milliseconds, Slack provides us with a URL which we can make a POST HTTP request to, much like how we sent webhook messages.

If your slash command does take longer than the maximum timeout and you're using the request URL, it is highly recommended that you return a message to Slack, letting the user know that their request is processing.

Replace the `http.createServer` block in your code with the following, noting the highlighted areas:

```
// create a simple server with node's built in http module
http.createServer((req, res) => {
    res.writeHead(200, {'Content-Type': 'text/plain'});

    // get the data embedded in the POST request
    req.on('data', (chunk) => {
      // chunk is a buffer, so first convert it to a string
      // and split it to make it legible
      console.log('Body:', chunk.toString().split('&'));

      let bodyArray = chunk.toString().split('&');
      let bodyObject = {};
```

```
    // convert the data array to an object
    for (let i = 0; i < bodyArray.length; i++) {
      // convert the strings into key value pairs
      let arr = bodyArray[i].split('=');
      bodyObject[arr[0]] = arr[1];
    }

    // if the token doesn't match ours, abort
    if (bodyObject.token !== SLACK_TOKEN) {
      return res.end('Invalid token');
    }

    // send a message immediately to confirm that
    // the request was receive it's possible that the
    // query will take longer than the time Slack waits
    // for a response (3000ms), so we'll send a
    // preliminary response and then send the results later
    res.end('Calculating response, be with you shortly!');

    // make sure to unescape the value so we don't get Unicode
    let query = unescape(bodyObject.text.split('+').join(' '));

    queryWolfram(query, (err, result) => {
    wolfram.query(message, (err, result) => {
      if (err) {
        console.log(err);
        return;
      }

      // send the result from the wolfram alpha request,
      // which probably took longer than 3000ms to calculate
      request
        .post(unescape(bodyObject.response_url))
        .send({
          text: result
        })
        .end((err, res) => {
          if (err) console.log(err);
        });
      });
    });
  }).listen(8080, '0.0.0.0');
```

After confirming that the slash command request came from our team, but before we even start the Wolfram Alpha API request, we return a confirmation message to the Slack channel letting the user know that their request is in the works.

Once Wolfram Alpha has returned our data, we send an HTTP POST request to the response URL provided to us in the slash command's initial request body. Let's try that last command again:

```
/wolfram distance between earth and moon
```

This should return a confirmation message:

Wolfram|Alpha bot BOT 15:23 Only you can see this message
Calculating response, be with you shortly!

A confirmation message lets the user know things are happening

A few seconds later, we should see the full result of the slash command query:

Our slash command returns an abundance of data

With our slash command working as expected, let's look at a quirk of the returned output.

In-channel and ephemeral responses

You might have noticed that when the Wolfram Alpha bot responds, it has the text **Only you can see this message** next to its name. As the text implies, the result of our bot is only visible to the user who initiated the slash command. This is an example of an ephemeral response. Note that the original slash command's text is also only viewable to the user that executed it. The opposite of ephemeral is an in-channel response, which can show both the slash command and result in the channel, for all to see.

By default, all slash command responses are set to ephemeral mode by the Slack API. Let's look at changing that and send in-channel messages instead. Once again, let's replace the contents of `http.createServer`. Go over the changes step by step:

```
// create a simple server with node's built in http module
http.createServer((req, res) => {
    res.writeHead(200, {'Content-Type': 'application/json'});
```

The main difference here is that we've changed the response's header content type to be `application/json`. This notifies Slack to expect a JSON package in string form.

The code is as follows:

```
// get the data embedded in the POST request
req.on('data', (chunk) => {
    // chunk is a buffer, so first convert it to a string
    // and split it to make it legible
  console.log('Body:', chunk.toString().split('&'));

  let bodyArray = chunk.toString().split('&');
  let bodyObject = {};

  // convert the data array to an object
  for (let i = 0; i < bodyArray.length; i++) {
    // convert the strings into key value pairs
    let arr = bodyArray[i].split('=');
    bodyObject[arr[0]] = arr[1];
  }

  // if the token doesn't match ours, abort
  if (bodyObject.token !== SLACK_TOKEN) {
    return res.end(JSON.stringify({
```

```
    response_type: 'ephemeral',
    text: 'Invalid token'
  }));
}
```

Our error response now requires that it be in stringified JSON format. Also, we add the response type `ephemeral`, which means that the error message will only be visible to the user who initiated the slash command:

```
// send a message immediately to confirm that
// the request was receive it's possible that the
// query will take longer than the time Slack waits
// for a response (3000ms), so we'll send a
// preliminary response and then send the results later
res.end(JSON.stringify({
  response_type: 'in_channel',
  text: 'Calculating response, be with you shortly!'
}));
```

Now, we specifically want an `in-channel` response. In this context, it means that both the slash command and the processing response will be visible to all in the channel:

Both the original slash command and the interim response are visible

And finally we query **Wolfram | Alpha**:

```
// make sure to unescape the value so we don't get Unicode
let query = unescape(bodyObject.text.split('+').join(' '));

queryWolfram(query, (err, result) => {
  if (err) {
    console.log(err);
    return;
  }

  // send the result from the wolfram alpha request,
  // which probably took longer than 3000ms to calculate
```

```
request
  .post(unescape(bodyObject.response_url))
  .send({
    response_type: 'in_channel',
    text: result
  })
  .end((err, res) => {
    if (err) console.log(err);
  });
 });
});
}).listen(8080, '0.0.0.0');
```

Here, we again ensure that the Wolfram Alpha result is visible to the entire channel. Finally, let's make some improvements to the display of the data in our `queryWolfram` function:

```
function queryWolfram(message, done) {
  wolfram.query(message, (err, result) => {
    if (err) {
      return done(err);
    }

    // if the query didn't fail, but the message wasn't understood
    // then send a generic error message
    if (result.queryresult.$.success === 'false') {
      return done(null, 'Sorry, something went wrong, please try
      again');
    }

    let msg = [];

    for (let i = 0; i < result.queryresult.pod.length; i++) {
      let pod = result.queryresult.pod[i];

      // print the title in bold
      msg.push(`*${pod.$.title}:*\n`);

      for (let j = 0; j < pod.subpod.length; j++) {
        let subpod = pod.subpod[j];

        for (let k = 0; k <subpod.plaintext.length; k++) {
          let text = subpod.plaintext[k];
          if (text) {
```

```
          // add a tab to the beginning
          msg.push('\t' + text + '\n');
        } else {
          // text is empty, so get rid of the title as well
          msg.pop();
        }
      }
    }
  }

  // join the msg array together into a string
  done(null, msg.join(''));
  });
}
```

Improvements here include bolding the title of a section and removing sections that have no text associated.

Now that we've put it all together, let's test it out:

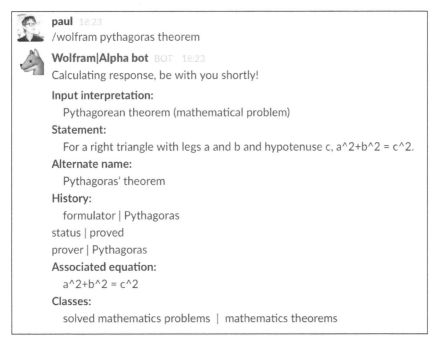

Wolfram Alpha can also be used to get definitions of popular algorithms

Bear in mind that slash commands are available universally in your Slack team. In our case, it means that the **Wolfram | Alpha** bot can be triggered from any channel, DM, or private group.

Using webhooks and slash commands

Now that we have a firm grasp on what webhooks and slash commands are, we should establish when to use them. First, we should consider when we'd use a webhook or slash command over a bot user, which we've learnt to build in previous chapters.

A bot user generally operates on a one-to-one basis; every bot requires a Slack token unique to that bot, meaning that the bot can only interact with the team associated with that token. This also allows the bot to maintain a real-time messaging connection with Slack and to reconnect in case of connection failure. Webhooks and slash commands, on the other hand, exist as external services and can be reused by many teams. By removing the need for a Slack token, you open up your app to be used by many other teams.

Use this flowchart to decide whether a webhook or a slash command is best for your needs:

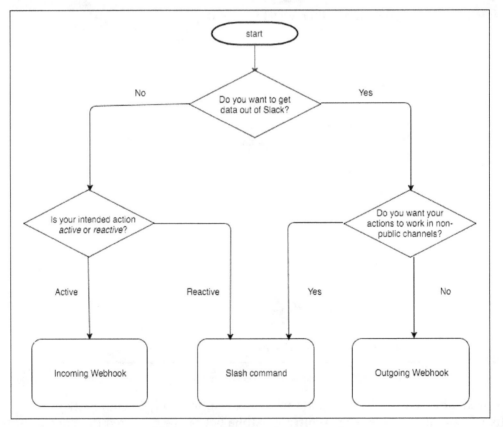

When to use webhooks or slash commands

In the preceding diagram, we mention the concepts of **active** and **reactive**. We covered these concepts back in *Chapter 3*, *Adding Complexity*, but the basic gist is that active apps and bots post messages without requiring input, whereas reactive bots respond to stimuli in the form of user input.

Summary

In this chapter, we saw what webhooks are and how to set them up to send data out of Slack and get data into Slack through a third-party server. We also discussed slash commands and how to implement them.

In the next chapter, we will cover how to publish your app so that other teams can make use of your bots, webhooks, and slash commands.

7
Publishing Your App

At this point, you have all the knowledge needed to build a bot that can increase your productivity and improve communications across teams. Hopefully, by now you have already thought of an idea for a bot that will not just make your own life easier but may also be useful for others. In this chapter, you will learn how to make your bot accessible to users outside of your own team and across the Slack community.

We will cover the steps necessary to add your bot to the Slack app directory and to make it accessible to others. We will review the following steps to add your bot onto the Slack app directory:

- Registering your bot and obtaining tokens
- Understanding the OAuth process
- Configuring the **Add to Slack** button
- Scopes
- Submitting your app or bot to the app directory
- Monetizing your bot

The Slack app directory

In order to make adding apps easy for their users, Slack has created the app directory (`https://slack.com/apps`). This is a place to shop for apps and bots to add to your Slack team. Like other app stores available, every app submitted to the app directory is controlled and has to be approved by Slack itself to counteract spam and abuse.

It is possible for other teams to use your bot by means of webhooks, as we saw in the previous chapter. However, if you are trying to reach a wide audience and potentially monetize your bot, the app directory is the most efficient way.

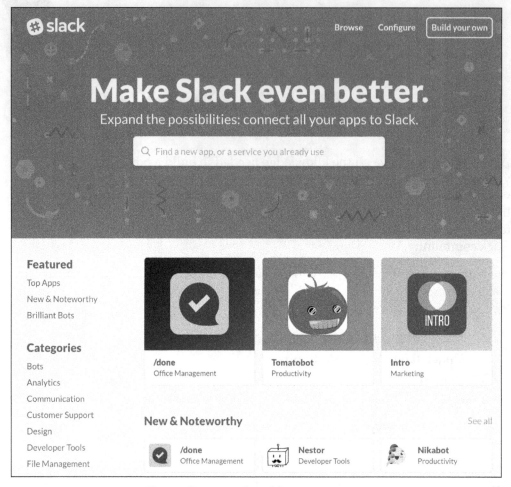

The app directory makes adding new apps easy

The end goal of this chapter is to allow users to add a bot to their Slack team by clicking an **Add to Slack** button, which we will cover in detail later.

Let's start by registering an app. In this example, we will add the *Wikibot* bot, which we built in *Chapter 3, Adding Complexity*.

Please note that our registering of Wikibot (and the use of the Wikipedia API) is for demonstrative purposes only. Always check the terms and conditions of a third-party API before using it for a bot you intend to publish. In the case of Wikibot, for example, we can use the Wikipedia API but aren't allowed to publish a bot named Wikipedia bot, as we do not own the trademark.

Registering your app and obtaining tokens

Certain unique tokens are required in order to successfully authenticate with Slack's OAuth servers. This is necessary so that Slack can determine whether we are who we say we are and whether our app or bot is actually integrated with the team we are attempting to get access to.

We start by navigating to the Slack new app registration page at `https://api.slack.com/applications/new`. Fill out the form by picking a name for your bot, the team it originated from, descriptions of your bot, links to help pages, and a redirect URI:

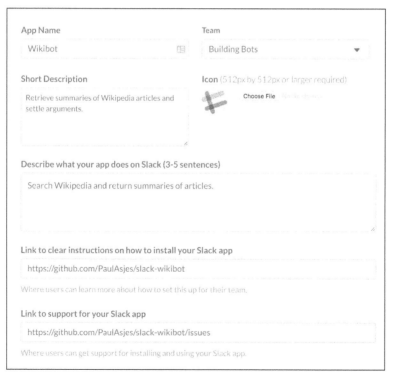

Be as descriptive as you can when filling out this form

After saving your settings, you can choose to set up a bot user, webhook, or slash command. For Wikibot, we will be setting up a bot user.

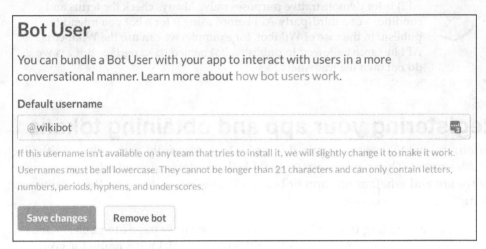

If your specified username is taken, Slack will edit it slightly to avoid conflicts

Once you've saved your changes, you should be presented with OAuth information on the next screen. First, make sure to save the **Client ID** and **Client Secret** codes from this page before moving on:

Never share your client secret with anyone

This process does not make your bot visible to the entire Slack user base; it simply registers your intent to develop an app. You will be able to test your app through the OAuth process. We will cover how to submit your bot to the app directory in a later section.

Understanding the OAuth process

In order to implement a bot user in a team that is not our own, we require a bot token similar to the ones we created earlier for our own team. We can request this token, but first we must prove that we are who we say we are using the OAuth process. **OAuth (Open Authentication)** is an open standard for authentication used by many companies, large and small.

The authentication process works through the following steps:

1. The user clicks the **Add to Slack** button.

2. Slack sends a request to the redirect URI provided in our app's settings page.

3. Once the request is received on our server, we redirect it to the authorization API endpoint (`https://slack.com/oauth/authorize`) and include the following parameters in the query string:

   ° `client_id`: This is the unique ID given to us when we first created our app.

   ° `scope`: This includes the permissions we require for our app. We will go into more detail on scopes later in this chapter.

   ° `redirect_uri`: This is an optional parameter. This is the URI that Slack will send the authorization results to. If left blank, the `redirect_uri` specified in the app settings page is used.

   ° `State`: This is a string we create; it could contain data we wish to preserve or function as our own identification method. For example, we could populate this field with a secret phrase that only we know, which we can later use to ensure that this request came from a trusted source.

   ° `Team`: This is the Slack team ID we wish to restrict our application to. This is useful when debugging our integration.

4. Slack sends a HTTP GET request to the redirect URI provided in our previous request. If absent, it defaults to the URI we provided in our app's settings page. The request contains the following parameters:

   ° code: This is a temporary code generated by Slack, and it is used to confirm our identity

   ° state: This is the string we created earlier, and it can be used to make sure this request is legitimate

5. Armed with all the tools and codes we need, we make a request for a bot user token from Slack in another HTTP GET request, passing the following parameters:

   ° client_id: This is the unique client ID given to us in the app's settings page

   ° client_secret: This is the unique and secret ID given to us in the app's settings page

   ° code: This is the code given to us by the request in step 4

   ° redirect_uri: This must match the previous redirect_uri if one was sent; otherwise, it is optional

6. Finally, if all went well, we will receive a response from Slack with all the data we require. It should look something like this:

```
{
  ok: true,
  access_token: 'xoxp-xxxxxxxxxxx-xxxxxxxxxxx-xxxxxxxxxxx-
  xxxxxxxxxx',
  scope: 'identify,bot',
  user_id: 'Uxxxxxxxx',
  team_name: 'Building Bots',
  team_id: 'Txxxxxxxx',
  bot: {
    bot_user_id: 'U136YALCW',
    bot_access_token: 'xoxb-xxxxxxxxxxx-
    xxxxxxxxxxxxxxxxxxxxxxx'
  }
}
```

To make this a bit easier to understand, let's look at a chart of these transactions:

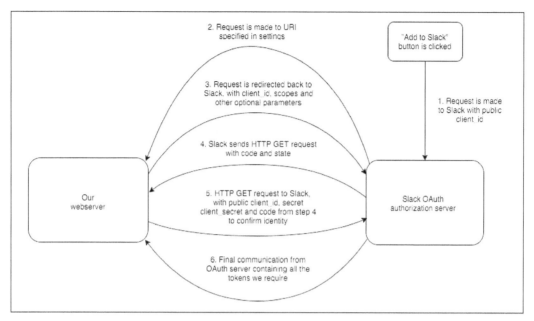

Slack's OAuth authorization procedure

Now, let's look at the preceding code example. In order to make our lives a bit easier, we will use the Express web framework (http://expressjs.com/) and the familiar superagent AJAX library. Make sure to install both by using the following command:

```
npm install -save express superagent
```

Next, let's put our server together; create or reuse an index.js file and paste the following code:

```
const request = require('superagent');
const express = require('express');

const app = express();

const CLIENT_ID = 'YOUR_CLIENT_ID';
const CLIENT_SECRET = 'YOUR_CLIENT_SECRET';

app.get('/', (req, res) => {
  res.redirect(`https://slack.com/oauth/authorize?client_id=${
  CLIENT_ID}&scope=bot&redirect_uri=${escape('http://YOUR_
  REDIRECT_URI/bot')}`);
});
```

```
app.get('/bot', (req, res) => {
  let code = req.query.code;

  request
    .get(`https://slack.com/api/oauth.access?client_id=${
    CLIENT_ID}&client_secret=${CLIENT_SECRET}&code=${code}&
    redirect_uri=${escape('http://YOUR_REDIRECT_URI/bot')}`)
    .end((err, res) => {
      if (err) throw err;
      let botToken = res.body.bot.bot_access_token;
      console.log('Got the token:', botToken);
    });

  res.send('received');
});

app.listen(8080, () => {
  console.log('listening');
});
```

The highlighted areas indicate where you should fill in your own tokens and URIs.

> It is highly recommended to use a service such as ngrok in order for your locally started server to be accessible from the Internet. Visit https://ngrok.com/ for more details and setup instructions. You should use ngrok only for development purposes. In production, you should use a dedicated server.

Navigate to the Slack button documentation page (https://api.slack.com/docs/slack-button#button-widget) and scroll down till you see the following test interface:

You can use this area to test that your integrations authenticate properly

Click on the **Add to Slack** button and you should be presented with a screen that asks you to confirm whether you'd like to authorize your bot for use in your channel. Click on the **Authorize** button and switch over to your terminal. The bot token we need will show up in a log:

```
listening
```

```
Got the token: xoxb-37236360438-xxxxxxxxxxxxxxxxxxxxxxxx
```

We can use our token to start our bot user and have it respond to and interact with users from other teams. Let's do that with Wikibot now. We will take the Wikibot code featured earlier in this book and alter it to function with the OAuth procedure outlined before. Replace the contents of index.js with the following:

```
'use strict';

const Bot = require('./Bot');

const wikiAPI = 'https://en.wikipedia.org/w/api.php?format=json&
action=query&prop=extracts&exintro=&explaintext=&titles=';
const wikiURL = 'https://en.wikipedia.org/wiki/';

const request = require('superagent');
const express = require('express');

const app = express();

const CLIENT_ID = 'YOUR_CLIENT_ID';
const CLIENT_SECRET = 'YOUR_CLIENT_SECRET';

app.get('/', (req, res) => {
    res.redirect(`https://slack.com/oauth/authorize?client_id=$
    {CLIENT_ID}&scope=bot&redirect_uri=${escape('http://[YOUR_
    REDIRECT_URI]/bot')}`);
});

app.get('/bot', (req, res) => {
  let code = req.query.code;

  request
    .get(`https://slack.com/api/oauth.access?client_id=$
    {CLIENT_ID}&client_secret=${CLIENT_SECRET}&code=${code}&
    redirect_uri=${escape('http://[YOUR_REDIRECT_URI]bot')}`)
    .end((err, result) => {
      if (err) {
        console.log(err);
```

```
        return res.send('An error occured! Please try again
        later');
      }
      console.log(res.body);

      let botToken = result.body.bot.bot_access_token;
      console.log('Got the token:', botToken);

      startWikibot(result.body.bot.bot_access_token);

      res.send('You have successfully installed Wikibot! You can
      now start using it in your Slack team, but make sure to
      invite the bot to your channel first with the /invite
      command!');
    });
  });

app.listen(8080, () => {
  console.log('listening');
});

function startWikibot(token) {
  const bot = new Bot({
    token: token,
    autoReconnect: true,
    autoMark: true
  });

  // The rest of the familiar Wikibot code follows.
  // Visit https://github.com/PaulAsjes/BuildingBots for the
  // complete source code
}
```

Let's try this out. Run the Node application after making sure that your `client_id`, `client_secret`, and `redirect_uri` are inserted in the highlighted sections of the preceding code. To test the integration, navigate to the documentation on the **Add to Slack** button here: `https://api.slack.com/docs/slack-button#button-widget`. As before, scroll down till you see the test widget, tick the **bot** box, and click on the **Add to Slack** button.

Below this test widget is the embed code you should use when placing the **Add to Slack** button on your website.

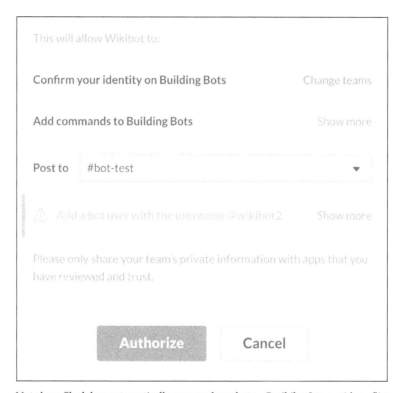

Note how Slack has automatically renamed our bot to @wikibot2 to avoid conflict

Once authorized, you should see the following message:

You have successfully installed Wikibot! You can now start using it in your Slack team, but make sure to invite the bot to your channel first with the /invite command!

We returned a simple string in this example. As per best practices, we need to redirect to a web page with some instructions on how to operate Wikibot.

Switch to the Slack client and to the channel you'd like to incorporate Wikibot. As we discussed in *Chapter 2, Your First Bot*, bot users have to be manually invited to a channel, so let's do that and test our bot:

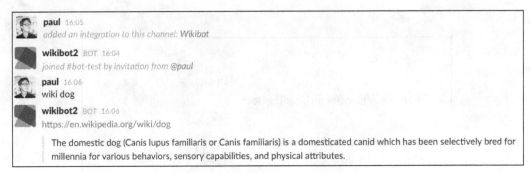

Our bot is successfully integrated and working!

Wikibot will now continue to function as long as our Node service is running.

Next, we will look at the other scopes available for our use.

Scopes

OAuth scopes allow you to specify exactly what access your app needs to perform its functions. In the previous example, we requested the `bot` scope, which gives our bots access to all the actions a bot user can perform. For example, the `channels:history` scope gives us access to the channel's chat history and `users:read` allows us to access the full list of users in the team. There is a long list of scopes available (which you can review at `https://api.slack.com/docs/oauth-scopes`), but we will focus on the three most likely to be used scopes in our apps:

- `bot`: This provides a bot token, allowing us to connect to the team as a bot user
- `incoming-webhook`: This provides an incoming webhook token
- `commands`: This provides a Slack token, which we can use to ensure that the incoming slash command requests are valid

 Scopes of the bot variety automatically include a subset of other scopes needed for the bot to perform. For more information, visit `https://api.slack.com/bot-users#bot-methods`.

Multiple scopes can be requested without issue. Here's an example of the bot, incoming webhook and command scopes being requested in our initial redirect:

```
app.get('/', (req, res) => {
  res.redirect(`https://slack.com/oauth/authorize?
  client_id=${CLIENT_ID}&scope=bot+incoming-
  webhook+commands&redirect_uri=${escape
  ('http://YOUR_REDIRECT_URI/bot')}`);
});
```

Note how the requested scopes are separated with a + symbol. This will return the following object after we authenticate:

```
{
  ok: true,
  access_token: 'xoxp-xxxxxxxxxxx-xxxxxxxxxxx-xxxxxxxxxxx-
  xxxxxxxxxx',
  scope: 'identify,bot,commands,incoming-webhook',
  user_id: 'Uxxxxxxxx',
  team_name: 'Building Bots',
  team_id: 'Txxxxxxxx',
  incoming_webhook:
    { channel: '#bot-test',
      channel_id: 'Cxxxxxxxx',
      configuration_url:
      'https://buildingbots.slack.com/services/xxxxxxxxx',
      url: 'https://hooks.slack.com/services/
      Txxxxxxxx/Bxxxxxxxx/xxxxxxxxxxxxxxxxxxxxxxxx' },
  bot:
    {
      bot_user_id: 'Uxxxxxxxx',
      bot_access_token: 'xoxb-xxxxxxxxxxx-xxxxxxxxxxxxxxxxxxxxxxxx'
    }
}
```

 Instead of using the + symbol, scopes can also be comma separated.

We now have all the pieces we need to create a bot (the `bot_access_token`), an incoming webhook (the `url` parameter in the `incoming_webhook` object), and the `access_token` we use for slash commands.

Submitting your app to the app directory

Once you have tested your integration within your team's channel, and you are happy with your bot, it's time to submit it to the app directory. To do so, first ensure that your application conforms to Slack's checklist for deploying an app (`https://api.slack.com/docs/slack-apps-checklist`). In short, your app must:

- Request only those scopes that are actually in use.
- Display the **Add to Slack** button on a webpage. You are required to have your own website with instructions and help for new users.
- Have an appropriate name (for example, no trademark or copyright infringement).
- Have an app or bot icon that is clear and distinctive.
- Have a high-quality icon that is at least 512 x 512 pixels in size.
- Include short and long descriptions of your bot's actions.
- Include an installation link (this can simply be a webpage displaying the **Add to Slack** button and a guide on how to use your bot).
- Feature an customer support link and e-mail, in case users run into problems installing your bot.
- Include a link to a privacy policy. Your bot could potentially be listening on private conversations, so you will need to specify exactly what data your bot will be collecting (if any).
- Have correct formatting and spelling. Your bot should use clear language and not contain any errors.

Note that our example, Wikibot, fails the *appropriate name* clause, as Wikipedia is clearly a registered trademark to which we do not own the rights. On this basis alone, Wikibot would be rejected.

Once you have confirmed that your app or bot conforms to the previous points, you can submit your application for review at `https://api.slack.com/submit`.

Like other app stores, a review process is mandatory for all new submissions. The length of the review period is highly dependent on the complexity of your app and on the quantity of submissions the Slack admissions team has to process.

 When you are ready to publish your app to the Slack app directory, you require hosting. A great way to get your bot up and running quickly is to use Beep Boop `https://beepboophq.com/`. A paid service, Beep Boop will host your Slack bots for you so you can focus on developing rather than infrastructure.

To ensure that your bot reaches your intended audience, consider submitting it to useful websites such as Botwiki (`http://botwiki.org`), botlist (`http://botlist.co`), and Product Hunt (`http://www.producthunt.com`) in order to get maximum exposure.

Monetizing your bot

Monetizing your bot, of course, is entirely optional and how you monetize it is dependent on the function of your bot and whether there is a market. Bear in mind that if your goal is to sell your bots for a one-off price, the Slack app directory does not support monetary transfers.

All apps in the app directive are free to install, but how you convert your user base to paying customers is left up to you.

There are a variety of methods to do this and there is no single correct way or Slack-*sanctioned* method. A popular method employed by companies such as Zoho Expense (`https://www.zoho.com/us/expense/slack-integration/`) is a payment plan based on users. The service is free for small teams, but once you require more than three users to have access, you have to migrate to a paid tier.

The idea here is similar to APIs we have encountered, such as Wolfram Alpha. This means using a tiered approach where a free tier exists (tied either to amount of calls made or an expiration date), but paid tiers are optional if more requests are needed.

Remember that when attempting to monetize your bot, the "try before you buy" sales tactic is key here. Users are unlikely to convert into paying customers if they don't have an idea of how your bot works and whether it is actually beneficial for them. Consider having either a free trial period or a free tier with limited functionality.

Above all, the most important aspect is ensuring that you have a product that is truly worth paying for. As useful as our *to-do* bot from *Chapter 4, Using Data* is, it's unlikely that anyone would pay money for such a simple bot, as free alternatives are readily available or easily recreated.

Therefore, the focus of your bot should be the solving of a particular problem first and monetizing a distant second.

Summary

In this chapter, you saw how to make your app accessible to other teams via the Slack App Directory. You saw how to request scopes from Slack to ensure that your apps have the correct permissions to perform actions. Finally, you learned how to correctly authenticate your apps with Slack and obtain the tokens required to make your bots, webhooks, and slash commands work.

By following the lessons in this book, you have obtained all the knowledge and tools required to create a world-class Slack bot. It is now up to you to create the next leap forward in bot technology and to push the boundaries of how we interact with bots to solve problems and achieve optimum efficiency.

To perhaps inspire you further, you should be aware that chat bots in general and Slack bots in particular are enjoying an unprecedented explosion in popularity and recognition.

At the beginning of his keynote speech at the 2016 Microsoft Build developers conference, Microsoft CEO Satya Nadella prophesized the future of bots:

> *"Bots are the new apps. People-to-people conversations, people-to-digital assistants, people-to-bots and even digital assistants-to-bots. That's the world you're going to get to see in the years to come."*

His argument is an intriguing one: that bots will potentially replace apps as the main source of communication between a company and their clients.

Facebook has also seen the potential in bots. In April 2016, they announced bots for their Messenger Platform, which is expected to see tremendous activity in the coming months and years.

Although this book focused on building bots specifically for the Slack platform, the techniques, best practices, and theory are all valid for any bot platform. Armed with this knowledge, you have everything you need to become a competent developer in this new bot revolution.

Happy coding!

Further reading

In this book, we used the Node Slack client directly to build our bots. Following this package on GitHub is the best way of staying up to date with new features and changes in the Slack ecosystem. There are, however, alternatives to using the official Node Slack client. Botkit (`https://github.com/howdyai/botkit`) is a fantastic package meant to abstract away a lot of the underlying concepts and streamline the bot creation process. Botkit also supports creating bots for Facebook Messenger for easy cross-platform bot development. If you wish to bootstrap the creation of your bot and get it up and running as soon as possible, consider using Botkit.

Index

A

access
  restricting 31-33
Add to Slack button
  URL 154
admins
  adding 33
  removing 33
  URL 33
app
  deploying, URL 158
  registering 147-149
  registration, URL 147
  submitting, to app directory 158
app directory
  about 145-147
  app, submitting 158
application program interface (API) 2, 39
asynchronous 68
authenticated event 25
authorization API endpoint
  URL 149

B

Beep Boop
  URL 158
bot
  commands 46-48
  connecting 69, 70
  debugging 33-37
  inputs, sanitizing 49-52
  monetizing 159
bot, building
  about 6

bot, connecting 16, 17
channel, joining 17, 18
channels. getting 19, 21
development tools installing,
    NPM used 7, 8
members, getting in channel 21-23
message, sending to channel 18, 23, 24
new project, creating 8-13
Node.js, installing 6, 7
Slack API token, creating 14-16
slack object 18, 19
botlist
  URL 159
Botwiki
  URL 159

C

channel
  getting 19
  joining 17, 18
  members, getting 21-23
  message, sending 18-24
classifiers
  about 108, 109
  trained classifiers, using 109-115

D

data
  displaying, in natural way 100
  retrieving 68, 69
  saving 68, 69
Dice coefficient 97
direct message (DM)
  sending 30, 31
dynamic storage 70-72

E

entities 114
ES6 6
ES2015 6
Express web framework
  URL 151
external API integration
  about 52-61
  error handling 61, 62

H

hashes 73, 74
Hubot
  URL 3
Hypertext Transfer Protocol (HTTP) 53

I

in channel
  and ephemeral responses 138-141
incoming webhooks
  about 120-124
  URL 120
inflection 99, 100
Internet Protocol (IP) 126
iron-node
  URL 33

J

Jaro-Winkler 97
JavaScript Object Notation (JSON) 8, 54

K

keywords
  classes, using 39-42
  reactive bots 43-46
  responding to 39

L

latency
  URL 77
Levenshtein distance 97
lists 75

M

Matt Jones
  URL 117
mentions 105-107
message event
  using 25-27
Mozilla Developer Network (MDN) 41

N

Natural
  URL 90
natural language processing (NLP)
  about 88-90, 134
  fundamentals 91
  generation 115, 116
  uses 103, 104
natural language toolkit (NLTK)
  URL 90
ngrok
  URL 126
Node ES6 guide
  URL 6
Node.js (Node)
  installing 6
nodemon
  URL 7
Node Package Manager (NPM)
  used, for installing development tools 7
node-wolfram
  URL 131

O

OAuth (Open Authentication)
    process 149-156
OAuth (Open Authentication) scopes
  about 156, 157
  URL 156
Open Weather Map 100
outgoing webhooks
  about 125-129
  URL 125

P

Product Hunt
URL 159

Q

Query GeoParser
URL 113

R

reactive bots 43-46
Real Time Messaging (RTM) client 10
Real Time Messaging (RTM) platform 3
Redis
about 63, 64
best practices 77-82
client implementations, URL 64
client, URL 69
connecting to 66, 67
installing 64
simple to-do example 82-87
URL 64, 65
Redis, installing
on Mac OS X 65
on Unix 65, 66
on Windows 65
**representational state transfer (REST)
    service 53**
responses
about 25
authenticated event 25
message event, using 25-27
spam, avoiding 27-30

S

sets
about 75
sorted sets 76
Slack
about 1, 2
app directory 145-147
as platform 2-4
goals 4
URL 2, 145

Slack API token
creating 14-16
slash commands
about 129-138
and webhooks, using 142, 143
spam
avoiding 27-30
stemmers 94-96
string distance 97, 98

T

tokenizers
about 92, 93
URL 93
tokens
obtaining 147-149
trained classifiers
using 109-114
typing indicator 60

U

uncanny valley 116-118
Uniform Resource Link (URL) 54

W

webhooks
about 120
and slash commands, using 142, 143
incoming webhooks 120-125
outgoing webhooks 125-129
Wolfram Alpha
URL 129, 130

Z

Zoho Expense
URL 159

www.ingramcontent.com/pod-product-compliance
Lightning Source LLC
Chambersburg PA
CBHW060134060326
40690CB00018B/3871